EFFECTIVE
LEADERSHIP
FOR
TODAY'S CHURCH

BOOKS BY ARTHUR MERRIHEW ADAMS
Published by The Westminster Press

Effective Leadership
for Today's Church

Pastoral Administration

EFFECTIVE
LEADERSHIP
FOR
TODAY'S CHURCH

by
Arthur Merrihew Adams

W

22027

THE WESTMINSTER PRESS

Philadelphia

Scripture quotations from the Revised Standard Version
of the Bible are copyrighted 1946, 1952, © 1971, 1973
by the Division of Christian Education of the National
Council of the Churches of Christ in the U.S.A., and are
used by permission.

Book Design by Dorothy Alden Smith

First edition

Published by The Westminster Press®
Philadelphia, Pennsylvania

PRINTED IN THE UNITED STATES OF AMERICA

9 8 7 6 5 4 3 2 1

Library of Congress Cataloging in Publication Data

Adams, Arthur Merrihew.
    Effective leadership for today's church.

    Includes bibliographical references and index.
    1. Christian leadership. I. Title.
BV652.1.A3   254   77-27547
ISBN 0-664-24196-4

Contents

Introduction

The local church and its leaders deserve more help than
they have usually received. In God's plans for his family
there are no more strategic instruments than the pastors and leaders of the congregations. This viewpoint
seems to me soundly based in Scripture and supported
by the long experience of the church.

We owe a great deal to those who have seen the fire
of God in ordinary congregations, as it flamed for Moses
in the wilderness. The burning bush captured his attention and the rest of his life (Ex. 3:1–10). It has long stood
for the difficult people called Israel, and for the new
Israel—the church. What makes this ground holy is not
Moses nor any leader since, but God. He brings about
the deliverance from Egypt and the greater deliverance from the curse and power of sin through the cross.
But when the salvation is complete, the grateful multitude gathers by the sea of glass mingled with fire to join
in the Song of Moses and the Lamb (Rev. 15:2–4). The
song is about the great and marvelous works of God.
The inclusion of Moses' name says something about the
importance of human leadership in the church.

This book is designed for pastors and church officers.

Its purpose is to clarify their thinking about leadership in the church and to increase their effectiveness. The chapters developed slowly and were tested over and over again in seminars with pastors and church officers. This project was well on its way several years ago. The live encounter with working leaders, many of whom had years of experience, introduced questions and suggested subject areas which had to be explored. These dialogues have increased enthusiasm for the project and I am now grateful that I did not rush to press prematurely.

My conviction about the importance of leadership has been strengthened over twenty-eight years of service as a pastor in three very different congregations. From them I learned the wonderful things that go on in people who look ordinary. I saw what God could do in and through them. I soon recognized that to be effective, a church has to find the leadership which God has planted in unexpected places.

It was primarily a desire to share that insight and raise up a generation of pastors who might be used by God to open the floodgates of power that led me to a seminary ministry which has now lasted fifteen years. In addition to relationships in class with candidates for ordination, my position involves day-to-day interaction with hundreds of parishes, their pastors and officers, and the students working with them in field education assignments.

Weekends are often spent with official boards of congregations as they think through ways of meeting their leadership responsibilities. I have also conducted more than fifty seminars for pastors from every part of the United States and Canada. Other insights emerged as I worked as a consultant to the Priests Committee of the Roman Catholic Diocese of Trenton, New Jersey, and with elders of a presbytery who developed responsibility descriptions for church sessions and for pastors.

Not least important in the framing of these chapters is the fact that during the last five years I have discussed in small seminars hundreds of case presentations by pastors in a Doctor of Ministry program. These have dealt theologically and practically with almost every conceivable situation requiring leadership. A valuable resource in this activity was a total of eighteen years' experience as ministerial relations chairperson in three presbyteries. In the United Presbyterian Church this committee deals with the placement of ministers and the problems that arise in the lives of pastors and congregations. These congregations were small and large, in settings rural, town, suburban, and inner-city.

Early in my pilgrimage, I recognized the importance for the local church and for Christ's worldwide mission of the connectional bodies at district, regional, national, and international levels. My theology sees them as integral parts of the church. But even if they are not, we cannot get along without them. For me, this has meant an obligation to do my part in judicatories at each level. In these capacities, I have worked more than a little at a sound concept of ministry for today.

Beyond the church walls in one city, I worked with a group of citizens to found a council of social agencies. In another, I served as a county commissioner of human relations. For twenty-five years I have been a director of the Presbyterian Ministers Fund, an interdenominational company that specializes in meeting the needs of ministers and their families. These secular undertakings have brought insights into the problems of leadership I might easily have missed.

I am also deeply indebted to the persons with whom I have served. Among them are a score of ordained associates and a much larger number of staff members —not to speak of hundreds of laypersons. The things they have taught me—and sometimes their stories—are woven into the fabric of this book. This is true also of my associates in the faculty and administration of Princeton Theological Seminary, and of a growing company of scholars and consultants interested in leadership. Invaluable editorial assistance has been provided by Madeline Simpson, my administrative assistant at Princeton Seminary.

It is my hope that this book will be helpful to the individual pastor or church officer. It may also be used as a basis for discussions in successive board meetings, or furnish an outline for orienting newly elected officers. Committees and task forces may turn to it as they begin an undertaking or as they struggle with a secular assignment.

Jethro's administrative counsel (Ex. 18:13–26) was no substitute for Moses' gifts or divine call, but it increased his effectiveness and probably lengthened his useful life! It is my prayer that this small volume may do as much for you.

1

Faith: The Basic Qualification

Faith is the most important qualification of a leader. A commitment to something so strong that it shapes the leader's life is contagious.

This was true of Moses. When he became sure of God and of the divine intention, the people followed him. Before that conviction took hold of him, his efforts at deliverance called forth no followers. The Children of Israel tested his faith again and again, and when it held fast against all odds, they followed him all the way to Canaan, and in the process became the people he believed they would become.

In the history that follows, there is a dramatic illustration of the difference faith makes. The Israelites in Canaan moved slowly toward nationhood under the stimulus of individuals who were pygmies in the faith compared to Moses. Among them was a man named Eli, who was unable to pass his faith on to his sons because his position and his comforts became more important to him. His heirs, Hophni and Phineas, accepted the values he lived by rather than those he professed. They failed miserably when they attempted to lead the men of Israel against the Philistines, a bold sea people who held them in bondage. Phineas' wife died in childbirth when she heard the news of her husband's failure and death. She left behind, in the name she chose for her son, her estimate of the situation: "Icabod," "the glory is departed" (I Sam. 4:21). The irony was that Israel was on the edge of a golden age, with the great nations around her preoccupied with other concerns. All that was required was a succession of leaders with faith strong enough to galvanize the people.

The Philistines destroyed Shiloh, the happy valley loved by Eli and his sons, and in the process scattered the old priest's understudies. Samuel, one of these understudies, had a personal experience of God. This turned the embers of the old man's faith into a hot fire that glowed in Samuel's life and kindled faith in David, also. These two men had many human imperfections, but their faith created a nation and established a tradition which is still alive. At the outset, they faced all the problems confronted by Hophni and Phineas. Their faith made the difference.

Elijah's impact upon his contemporaries, and his lasting influence, are likewise rooted in the nature of his faith and the depth of his conviction. This is also true of Jeremiah, who performed the impossible task of keeping faith alive under conditions in which it could only endure failure and trouble. Jeremiah's faith still imparts courage in dark days and keeps pilgrims going when there is not a hint of relief in sight.

The calm assurance of the disciples of Jesus continues in this great tradition. They were attacked from many quarters, but no one doubted their sincerity or the depth of their conviction. The tight bond between their views and their lives gave projectile force to their leadership.

The same quality appears in the apostle Paul. Read again the Pauline letters and the book of Acts and ask: What made this man the spectacular leader he was? Why did people respond and gather into churches wherever he went? The answer is clear. It was his message, and the impact of a life utterly dedicated to it. There was no question about what the apostle believed or what it meant.

In a very different time this was also true of Bernard of Clairvaux. Before he was out of his teens, this son of well-to-do parents entered a monastery, located in a swamp and in imminent danger of closing for lack of both men and resources. Soon it was flourishing and overflowing with members, and Bernard was sent to establish a new house at Clairvaux, which was to become one of the most famous centers in Christendom. Kings and popes turned to Bernard for advice and hung on his words. He became one of the key leaders of his time. Why? There were persons more attractive and knowledgeable and politically adroit. This man had ruined his digestion by extreme asceticism, so that he rarely was able to keep all of a meal down, and he resolutely held to the quiet of his cloisters. The one thing he had was a strong faith—and this made him a leader.

We could say as much of Martin Luther and John Wesley and Martin Luther King, Jr., and a host of others, including pastors and church officers we have known.

The importance of conviction in leaders is, of course,

not limited to the realm of religion. Cyrus the Persian is a shadowy figure in antiquity, but we know that his vision for his people inspired fantastic loyalty. He could start out toward a trouble spot with a bodyguard of a dozen men and arrive at a battlefield, followed by a host of ten thousand who had rallied to his cause as he passed by. Thousands of years later George Washington, with limited knowledge and experience of warfare, often ill, and leading men who existed under intolerable conditions of cold and hunger and deprivation, kept an army in the field for years. He had an unshakable faith in political freedom which shaped his life and spilled over into the lives of his followers.

J. Douglas Brown, writing for leaders in education, social welfare, business, and industry, stresses the central importance of "intuitive integrity."[1] This is a deepset and consistent system of ideas and values, attitudes and goals which are so much a part of the leader as to affect behavior even when he or she is acting without conscious thought. Through the give-and-take of everyday experience, this perspective is communicated and becomes the driving force in a constituency.

The deep-seated and consistent faith permeating the thinking and guiding the action of the effective church leader is a conception of and relation to God and his family born of God's revelation of himself in his Son Jesus Christ. It involves a vivid awareness that God is bringing into being a family of millions to live in love with him and with each other now and forever. Stretching into eternity out of the past, joining hands around the world, God's family in each generation experiences and shares with others the grace revealed in Jesus Christ. Formed into units in particular locations by the

Spirit of God and endowed by him with essential gifts, the members of the family gather for worship and mutual nurture, and go forth in mission. As the Bible makes plain from Genesis to Revelation, the goal of the mission is a multitude like the stars which no man can number. (Gen. 12:1–3; 15:5; Isa. 63:15–16; Hos. 11:1; Matt. 6: 6–15; 12:50; Luke 15:1–32; John 1:12; Rom. 6:15; 8: 14–39; II Cor. 6:17–18; Gal. 3:26; 4:5–7; Eph. 2:9; 3: 14–21; Rev. 7:9–12.) They are to live with God and with each other here and always in love and concern for justice, in freedom and fulfillment. The first step is faith in God as the parental sort of person we meet in Jesus.

A man or a woman whose life is dominated by this faith has the intuitive integrity the church needs in its leaders. Faith is, of course, not sight, for no one has seen God at any time. All are subject to occasional doubting. Even experiences of the absence of God, which some have mistakenly perceived as evidences of his death, may prepare us for deeper levels of faith. The testimony of the saints about such experiences is too often neglected in our time. Fluctuations need not worry us. The important requirement is that conviction be powerful enough to give life its main thrust.

A GIFT FOR THE SEEKER

The faith we need is a gift of God. We cannot earn it or create it or make it strong by trying. We can seek it with the Savior's assurance that those who seek, find. Isaac, the son of Abraham, who sought water in the wells where his father had found it, suggests where one may look for faith (Gen. 26:18–19). The church is called "the mother of the faithful" because so many have received the gift of faith through the fellowship of believers. Belief may spring up through close contact with one believer over a period of time, through association with a worshiping community, or by way of involvement in a group working together for Christian ends. The Bible is called the Word of God because his Spirit has spoken to millions and quickened them to faith as they read. Prayer has proved to be an open door for others. Response to a crying need has more than once resulted in the committed one recognizing Christ as at once the person served and the inspiration of the action.

"Seeking" in our Lord's promise is wholehearted living up to the best clues life has to offer. Christ met Saul of Tarsus on the road to Damascus after that intense little man had turned his back on the comforts and security of the scholar's study to attack what he thought to be an evil. Belief came to Augustine after years of earnestly trying every promising key to meaning. The faith that swept England took hold of John Wesley following a succession of fruitless efforts to live up to the best that he knew, and a disastrous missionary journey that might have cost him his life. And in the parable of the friend at midnight, Jesus seems to be saying that the question God asks before bestowing the gift of faith is how much a person wants it (Luke 11:5–13).

Beyond the birth of faith in a leader comes its development. The wells that supplied living water for the thirsty outsider will continue to support the spiritual life of the believer, but only if he or she continues to draw on them. The pastor, church officer, or ecclesiastical official who becomes too busy for prayer or Bible-reading, or intimate fellowship, or modest acts of Christian compassion, may not be aware that faith is ebbing away, and with it the power to lead. Like the gift of life, faith requires daily nourishment. The food to sustain it and provide for its growth is there for the asking, but God will not force-feed us.

DEVELOPED THROUGH USE

Faith also shares with life a dynamic quality: it must be in constant use or it will atrophy. The early church soon discovered that the maintenance and development of faith required a continual dialogue with the world. Each day there are new questions about the meaning of the Christian story in particular situations, new areas of the self or the world which need to be baptized, and new denials of the truth as we understand it in Christ. To neglect these issues is to risk the subversion of faith or its total loss. One must become a theologian to remain a believer.

Christian leaders sometimes become so absorbed in other tasks that this crucial obligation is neglected. Hard wrestling with contemporary challenges does not happen. Daily, the believer is confronted with new data apparently inconsistent with the Christian world view. Hideous events grin at belief in ultimate love and victory over death. These shattering intrusions are not brought to the light or grappled with in round after round. Instead, they are pushed down out of sight. Out of sight—but not out of mind! They toss restlessly, festering in the subconscious. Then one day their weight is too much; the scales suddenly tip; the whole structure of belief is gone and seems beyond recovery. The leader goes on with the right words and acts, but there is no heart in them. It is all pointless.

The alternative is to take theology seriously and give it the priority it deserves. For the church officer, this means time set aside for Bible study, for meditation, and for reading books that deal with areas where the most pressing challenges to faith arise, or where daily decisions or new options cry out for Christian insight and direction. It involves insistence upon theological guidance from the pastor in sermons and conversations and in the give-and-take of administrative activity. For the pastor, it means a large block of every week devoted to wrestling with the principalities and powers in the air of the time—under the light of Biblical revelation, the history of the church in the world, and the best thought and distilled experience of Christians in all ages.

STRENGTHENED THROUGH DISCIPLINE

Both the church officer and the pastor soon learn that the obligation to deepen and extend the boundaries of faith and meet its obligations calls for discipline of a high order. Our Lord offered his followers a straight and narrow path, and his expectations have not changed (Matt. 7:13–14). He was not particularly interested in ascetic practices, but he was prepared to do without anything—or go through anything—to achieve the Father's purpose. His daily schedule had clear priorities. This he expected of his disciples. He needed leaders for his enterprise, and he knew that only the disciplined are prepared to lead.

The leaders we have described as persons of great

faith learned to discipline themselves, shaping their lives as an aerodynamics engineer shapes a rocket or a plane to move with the least possible resistance toward its objective.

The apostle Paul described his personal discipline as akin to that of an athlete. As we look at the trim bodies of Olympic contenders and observe the grace of their performances, it is easy to forget the hard training that kept their goals in sight. Remembering what it cost them to be where they are, we can form some estimate of its importance to them. When we read in *All the President's Men*[2] of the all-night vigils and endless hours of writing and correcting which Bernstein and Woodward put into one of their newspaper stories, inevitable comparisons arise. What would sermons be like if every pastor used that much energy on each one? What would church school classes be like if the teachers cared enough to spend themselves as these two newsmen did? What impact would the family of God be making on the world if its officers and members were carrying forward the mission with the self-denying intensity of the two investigative reporters?

More than once, working with a church member on an educational endeavor or an evangelistic enterprise, a visitation effort to nurture members, a project to relieve distress or change oppressive conditions, I have been conscience-stricken at the hours involved and the cost to individuals. Then I became aware of neighbors who were spending even more time perfecting a golf swing or a tennis shot. The issue became not the cost in discipline but the importance of the goal.

This is the issue raised by the call for discipline. A look

at a person's datebook and checkbook reveals what he or she believes, and the calendar is probably the more revealing of the two.

Employees in many businesses may occasionally be asked to keep a careful record for three weeks of the use of each half hour of the working day. The results of the first survey of this sort are often startling. Some companies have discovered that they could be more productive with 20 to 30 percent fewer workers. Surprises of the same magnitude often await an individual who keeps a record for three weeks of his or her use of time. Weekly charts are drawn with vertical columns for the seven days and horizontal columns for each hour or half hour of the waking day. Six or seven categories are developed for normal uses of time, each designated by a letter. Thus, a pastor might have the categories: D=Devotions; S=Study and Sermon Writing; R=Reading; P=Pastoral Calling and Counseling; M=Meetings; A=Administrative Activities such as planning, organizing, personnel, and small-group leadership; F=Free Time for family, meals, rest, and recreation. Once a three-week record is available, it is possible to begin experimenting with a time budget. This weekly chart offers an opportunity with the use of chosen categories to plan a disciplined use of time in terms of rational priorities derived from what you believe. Like all human schemes, such a time budget will be subject to change in the face of unexpected developments. But if followed consistently for even a few months, it will contribute substantially to the individual's capacity to shape life in terms of beliefs.

EXPANDED IN VISION

The Christian leader's preoccupation is not with the self but with God and God's vision for his family in the world. Everything else is made to serve that dream.

The Bible declares that "where there is no prophecy the people cast off restraint" (Prov. 29:18). The leader is expected to be a prophet in the sense that he or she is one who sees what is really there and calls it to the attention of those about. When the church falters, it is usually because the blind are leading the blind; there is no vision. The tragedy of our time is that we have people who can see into space well enough to land a man in a specific location on the moon, while we lack those who can see the dimensions of the spiritual universe well enough to create an atmosphere of love and trust and hope.

A leader must also have other qualifications, of course. But the evidence is overwhelming that more important than anything else—and indeed indispensable—is faith and the vision that accompanies it.

2

Sensitive Care for Persons

The caring person makes the best leader for the church. William Sloane Coffin, then chaplain at Yale University, once assured a group of seminarians at their baccalaureate service that caring for people, in addition to being a rich privilege in itself, would constitute a strong base for their leadership. He told of a pastor in a New England village, under attack for vigorous advocacy of social action, who was summoned to a congregational meeting called to consider his dismissal. The first speaker was the president of the local John Birch Society, who forcefully stated his opposition to the pastor's activities. Then he added: "The minister faithfully cared for my wife as she lay dying and has since supported me in the worst days of my life. If anyone tries to run the pastor out of the church, he will have to do it over my dead body!" The caring opened the door for further leadership.

This was true of Moses' experience. He loved the people of Israel and they knew it. Sometimes they exasperated him beyond endurance, but his concern always flared up again like an eternal flame. (Ex. 14:11–12; 15:24; 16:2; 17:2; 32:31–32.)

David's hold on his followers was cemented by strong ties of affection. In exile, he spoke with longing for the water of Bethlehem, and men risked their lives to get some for him; but he poured it out on the ground as an offering to God, rather than touch it to his lips, when he learned of the risks they had taken for him. Even in old age, he could go alone into harried exile and soon be surrounded by men who had served with him in other times. (II Sam. 23:15–17.)

We get some hint of Elijah's caring in the story of his tenderness toward the widow and her son. This man of blood and iron, moving through a largely hostile world with compelling force, could stare down a king or a queen. But he presented a very different face to the young prophets in his school and to the needy people around him. They knew he cared about them. (I Kings 17:1–24; II Kings 2:5–13.)

Our Lord's love lies at the very center of his being. He cares personally and particularly about each human being, and this is evident on virtually every page of the gospel record. It is his love which more than anything else binds each of us to him because, despite the cost, it binds him to us. Paul speaks for all of us when he says, "The love of Christ controls us, because we are convinced that one has died for all. . . . And he died for all, that those who live might live no longer for themselves but for him who for their sake died and was raised." (II Cor. 5:14–15.)

This love was explosive in Paul, as it moved into his life and through him into individuals and groups all over the known world. The apostle could be as hard as flint against any barrier to the gospel, but his affection for those he served shaped his prayers, his journeys, and his letters. It involved him in hardships and abuse. He knew that it evoked such a strong response that he could send a runaway slave back to his master, assured that instead of being flogged, Onesimus would be received as a brother. (Philemon 10–16.)

We have remarked upon the impact of Bernard's faith. In his case, too, intensity of conviction was matched by a deep affection for his followers. He really cared about each one, and gave evidence of this in individual attention and patient nurture and high expectations which forced growth. His faith drew men to him and what he believed; his love had a part in holding them fast.

This was true also of the Christian leaders we met in the first chapter. The facts are too well known to call for recital. It is also true of numberless pastors and church officers, and it has its analogue in the secular realm. Cyrus the Persian, like so many political leaders since, won the hearts of his followers by adding to his intense dedication to a national ideal a warmth of concern for individuals, unusual in his time. George Washington, by his complete identification with the suffering men encamped with him, won an undying place in the hearts of his countrymen.

DEVELOPING SENSITIVITY

Awareness of the importance of personal relationships in leadership has led to the extensive development of techniques for sensitizing those in training for leadership. People gather in small groups and are introduced to experiences designed to make participants more aware of their feelings and those of others. Attention is focused on the experienced behavior of members. Most educational strategies deal primarily with rational concerns. This approach focuses on the emotional life and encourages one to feel how emotions affect relationships with others. The gatherings may be called "T" (Training) groups, "L" (Learning) groups, encounter groups, or human relations laboratories. In them, tens of thousands of would-be leaders have discovered the importance of sensitivity to feelings.[3]

An awareness of feeling is not to be equated with Christian love. It may be used diabolically to manipulate persons, and many of us have seen skilled practitioners do just that. Their training enables them to reach over the rational faculties of people around them to induce action, as too many advertisers and politicians try to do, and as some people do intuitively. The sensitizing process has the virtue of making persons aware of this behavior and how it feels to be on the receiving end of manipulative efforts. This may be salutary or it may have little effect, except that they become more subtle in an effort to avoid alienating their victims. Quite a few do come to feel that any manipulative conduct designed to overcome the rationality of others is ultimately self-defeating. Their consciously directed behavior moves away from manipulation, but because the new approach is rooted in nothing deeper than utility, there is very limited effect on the intuitive behavior which governs a very large percentage of relationships.

Sensitivity training may be redeemed from futility by the sensitizing love we experience in Christ. For one who has begun the journey through the everlasting "no" to self, such training may suggest how far there is to go.

The Christian leader's sensitive caring involves attitudes toward human beings which have their roots in a continuing response to the love of God in Christ, which includes an entrance into his thoughts and feelings and attitudes. One thinks of the change in the attitude of Telemachus toward the familiar carnage of the gladiatorial games after he met Christ. A similar case is the costly revulsion toward human slavery experienced by John Newton, who had viewed its cruelties with equanimity until Jesus took hold of his life; or Wilfred Grenfell's sensitivity to the suffering of Labrador fishermen after he became a Christian.

CARING RESPECTS REASON

Sensitive caring makes room for reason. It respects the mind of the other person and avoids manipulation. Jesus himself built on the high anthropology of the Old Testament. This did not, like the Greeks, consider reason the supreme human faculty. That place was reserved for the capacity to commune with God. But even this experience assumes rationality, as does the consequent moral responsibility and eligibility for covenants. Further, the divine intention of establishing a kingdom held together, like a family, by love can only be viewed as nonsense if the members are not free to choose love or lovelessness. Our Lord would not bypass minds and manipulate people, though his unwillingness to do this led to a merciless flogging and a cross. It is shocking that a human being will do for small ends what God's Son would not do to avoid the cross or all the pain he shares with creation.

TO CARE IS TO FEEL

There is a feeling element in the sensitive caring of the Christian leader. When one comes to believe that God is in Christ, the full import of his love strikes home. The first response is, "He loves me; how incredible and wonderful." Where this is genuine, it is shortly followed with the realization: "He loves every one of the people around me. Each is a center of concern for him and must be for me."

This answering love we find welling up within us represents a shift in the center of our concern. Now, others share with ourselves the focus of attention. The change is far from complete, but at least some of the time we find ourselves noticing how others think and feel, instead of wondering first of all what they are thinking about us. This release from self-centeredness, which makes interpersonal sensitivity possible and worthwhile, is obviously a gift of God, flowing out of our experience of his love in Christ.

ON BEING OPEN TO OTHERS

There is also an experiential element in Christian sensitivity. Watch Jesus at work. See how much he exposes himself to the experiences of others. This is in the very nature of the incarnation. He goes where they are. He listens. He shares their joys and sorrows. He feels their pains and frustrations. He knows when they are hungry and tired. He senses their intentions.

The disciples develop the habit of empathy from him. Put them down anywhere and they soon know a lot about the men and women around them. Part of this is due to the consciousness which he nourishes that God is always present in human need. The rest of the world looks for God in victories and impressive achievements. Jesus says, "As you did it to one of the least of these my brethren, you did it to me" (Matt. 25:40). This imparts a new fascination to people in need. Note, however, that for Jesus and his disciples the sensitivity is not to a class or mass of people but to particular individuals. It is unfortunate that in the modern world we often lack knowledge of the persons around us. We frequently find ourselves gathered at a Communion table or a worktable trying to relate to a whole circle of unknown quantities.

Often, when a leader is meeting for the first time with a group of church officers, it is useful to devote time to an exercise in which those present share with the others one satisfying experience from childhood, one from youth, and one from adult years. The participants are fascinated by the stories, and are often surprised how interesting are the persons they have been working with for years. It is also remarkable how much easier it is for them to develop the mutual respect and trust so important in group enterprise. The goodwill generated in this way opens doors to better communication and better decisions. Further, a group that has reached this degree of experiencing each other is often ready for the next step of agreeing to visit in the homes of the congregation. They are prepared to move beyond the formal representation to which they were elected to introducing an incarnational type of Christian relationship.

LOVING THE UNLOVABLE

A sound personal knowledge of those with whom one works helps to shape one's caring and delivers it from being sentimental or impatient.

The biblical assertion that "all have sinned" takes on existential substance in close relationships, and the consequences for the leader become obvious. Caring becomes an exercise in limitless patience and repeated forgiveness. We see this vividly in the life of Moses. In his experience we are also reminded that the leader will fail at times because of inner sinfulness. Awareness of the sinfulness of all involved can deliver both leader and led from perfectionist dreams, while emphasizing their common dependence on the grace of God and teaching them to turn to him in crises.

In addition to the difficulties that arise from sinfulness, the leader has to deal with pressures created by ordinary human need and weakness. Freud[4] believed that folk sought in a leader the ideal father. According to this theory, people are looking for someone to take the place of the superego—the depository of parental injunctions—so they can escape anxiety about what they ought to do. Successors of Freud see the leader as one who meets a number of emotional needs. One need is a love object to whom they can give the devotion of which their parents were not quite worthy, and from whom they can expect caring they did not receive. Another is a symbol of the whole group who will be an exemplar of the group's standards and so deliver the members from fulfilling impossible ideals. Yet another is a scapegoat available when things go wrong.

The clue to handling these expectations may be found in the fact that Jesus Christ meets them. These deep needs which arise in every human being, insofar as they are legitimate—and there is a valid element in each of them—are to be met, not by the leader, but by Christ. The leader's task is to see that Jesus Christ gets the center of the stage. Our Lord will meet the sound need for a caring parent, a moral guide and example, a worthy love object, and a scapegoat; he will also reveal unhealthy impulses toward overdependency and irresponsibility.

Sensitive caring is not pandering to weakness or fostering it. The Christian leader should learn from his Master when support is needed and how it may be found in Christ and his church, corporate or individual. It will mean, among other things, effort to develop social structures and processes suitable for human beings who are not angels, so they can function when one or another falters or falls below the family standards.

The kind of understanding that develops from close personal attention to individuals also opens the door to sublime possibilities. There are furled wings in many of God's children. This challenges the leader to develop opportunities and arrangements that will enable and inspire individuals to spread their wings and bring blessings to themselves and to the world God loves.

The rest of the book represents an effort to suggest ways in which this may be accomplished by the caring leader.

3

The Leader's Authority

Authority is a kind of power. Before we focus on authority, we need to explore power and see how it affects motivation. Power itself is the capability of making things happen, and in organization this means the ability to see that persons act in certain ways. One of the problems facing persons with leadership responsibility is that the use of power to move people often alienates them. Freedom, conceived as the ability to act as one chooses, is a precious right and most people resist its violation. If power is to be effective, it must either override freedom or enlist it.

DIFFERENT KINDS OF POWER

Power strategies may be physical—based on superior bodily strength, or on a whip or a gun or a lock, enabling one person to override another's freedom. They may be utilitarian, securing compliance with money or things essential or desirable. They may be social (or normative), motivating action in response to personal advantages, such as distinction, prestige, position, or influence; or ideal benefactions, such as pride of accomplishment, a sense of adequacy, or an expression of religious feeling; or the satisfactions of communion, such as solidarity or belonging.

Physical strategies are plainly incompatible with the spirit of Jesus, who told Peter to put away his sword even in the face of lethal attack. Few contemporary churchmen are tempted to use force, and we are all embarrassed by memories of the Crusades, the Inquisition, and the burning of Servetus.

Utilitarian strategies present a more ambiguous issue. They are used when the church establishes employee relationships. This introduces complexities in motivation; for example, in a person who responds to God's call and serves out of love in a church vocation but is paid for services rendered. Certainly, the kind of service required of Christian leaders cannot be bought. The power to lift a congregation out of lackluster performance or despondency into praise, to put the stars back in a person's sky, to awaken a passion for justice or stir a people to love one another comes from the Spirit of God and cannot be poured into a leader by economic incentives. However, the professional religious leader who devotes all of each day to the task cannot exist without financial support. It is better for the individual and the church to face the fact that this means that utilitarian considerations will affect full-time workers and have some impact on the quality of what they do. A pastor who is worried about household expenses or the cost of educating children is likely to be hampered in the performance of ministry and to resent the sacrifices he or she is expected to make. On the other hand, the shepherd whose material recompense far exceeds that of many in his flock may also be handicapped.

Churches are only beginning to deal forthrightly with this subject.

The other side of the coin is the widely held opinion that the church cannot function like other institutions because most of its workers are volunteers. Persons attending administration seminars have been known to maintain that authority cannot be exercised—or that supervision is impossible—in the church because the people are not paid. It seems to be assumed that the only strong incentives are utilitarian. Since the church limits itself to social or normative inducements, except for a few employees, it cannot be expected to act corporately with much force.

This is sheer nonsense. Utilitarian incentives have less impact than is generally supposed if basic needs are being met. In a society like ours in which very few people are hungry or shelterless, social considerations have great weight even in the secular sphere. Business and industry are much aware that financial rewards, except as they are symbolic of social realities, rarely release creativity or produce dynamic teamwork. Christian action, individual and corporate, has its springs in gratitude and love for Christ—motives of great power. In a sense, lay workers in a church are not volunteers. The purposes of the church are not optional for Christians: to belong to Christ is to be engaged with him in mission. The individual needs the church for this just as much as the church needs the individual. Further, the ties of love which bind members to the church and set them under its authority have some of the primal force of those in the family. It was not utilitarian interests that enabled the early church to stand against imperial Rome, that gave the Reformers power to withstand the onslaught of pope and emperor, that moved the confessing German church to hold out against Hitler. The church is a voluntary organization in the sense that it relies primarily on social or normative incentives, but it differs from most voluntary societies in the strength of the motivations.

LEVELS OF MOTIVATION

Abraham Maslow has developed a theory of motivation based on a hierarchy of needs arranged in order of their emergence.[5] He argues that we pursue the gratification of these needs in a particular order. As gratification is achieved, a need ceases to have influence on behavior. The order is as follows: (1) physiological needs (food, warmth, elimination, sex); (2) safety (security and freedom from fear); (3) social (belonging); (4) self-esteem; and (5) self-realization (fulfillment). The fifth set is never adequately met. It may be worth noting that faith in action results in self-realization, though not directed to this end.

M. Scott Myers, of Texas Instruments, Inc., proposes a simple framework of two basic levels.[6] He calls the first "maintenance needs" and observes that if these are not met, a person is dissatisfied and will probably be ineffective. But, he warns, improvement in the maintenance area will not result in more highly motivated behavior. This may be surprising, since virtually all of Maslow's first three classifications are included in the maintenance category. Myers designates the higher level "motivational needs," and includes here opportunity for growth, achievement, responsibility, and recognition. The presence of opportunity to meet these needs seems to produce highly motivated behavior.

Myers' findings suggest that leaders in the church need to be sure that as far as possible the members are protected against the dissatisfactions of poor maintenance. These are likely to be present if the church supplies workers with inadequate equipment, develops little sense of belonging, fails to clarify expectations or express appreciation, and distributes status with an uneven hand. Even more important, the church must provide opportunities for meaningful work clearly related to its mission. Such work should be of sufficient importance to be worth the time and effort required, and suited to the particular gifts of the Holy Spirit to each individual, including aptitude, knowledge, and skills. Responsibility for decisions about projects will be there for the taking and the worker will sense that the tasks hold potential for personal growth and development.

Douglas McGregor, in *The Human Side of Enterprise,* observes that in business and industry leaders function with one of two contrasting assumptions about people which he calls "Theory X" and "Theory Y."[7] According to "Theory X," the average human being dislikes work and can be expected to work only if offered a carrot or threatened with a stick—or both. He or she prefers security and direction to responsibility. "Theory Y" assumes that the expenditure of physical and mental effort in work is as natural as in play. A person will exercise self-direction and self-control in the service of objectives regarded as worthwhile. Commitment to a task and a sense of responsibility develop when they are seen as means to the achievement of goals that appear important to the worker. Goals take on importance when one has a part in deciding what they are to be or helps in establishing the process by which they are de-cided. There is a remarkably wide diffusion among the population of imagination and creativity which can be drawn upon when participation in goal-setting opens the way to commitment.

McGregor's "Theory Y" should not be a difficult as-sumption for anyone who takes seriously the biblical view of human beings as children of the Creator. In view of their inheritance, we would expect them to like work in the service of the Father's ends. When they seem reluctant it may be useful to ask why. Biblical history suggests that one reason is sin—the rebellious stance which disposes us to place ourselves at the center of things instead of God, and prefer our own ends to his. The Christian leader is not surprised when this happens among colleagues in church. Fellow Christians have been induced by the love of God in Christ to repent and establish God at the center of their lives so that his purposes reign supreme. Yet day after day they keep disclosing areas of their lives not quite turned around. In all the members of the body of Christ are vestiges of the old cancerous impulses to follow independent goals. Part of leadership will always be earnest prayer for fel-low workers, and efforts to keep them in touch with the means of grace ordinarily used by the Holy Spirit to develop in each child of God the ever-increasing love of the Father and his family which moves the body forward in unity.

Another obligation of Christian leaders is to ask our-selves whether a "Theory Y" assumption about those around us could lead to stronger motivation for service. Often I am told that it is difficult in a particular congre-gation to secure board members or church school teachers or committee members. The obvious questions are suggested by Myers' categories and McGregor's insight about the marriage of commitment on the one hand and, on the other, participation in the decision-making which shapes the tasks. In too many churches a few people call the tune and wonder why others will not dance.

When there is difficulty in recruiting workers, or lackluster performance by church leaders, we need also to ask the deeper question about the communication of faith and the development of love. The theories of motivation we have been exploring make it clear that God has so arranged the universe that our needs are met in doing his will. These needs cannot be ignored, but the real pressure on us to serve is the love of Christ and our answering affection. Faith and love are very powerful. Maslow's motivational hierarchy simply does not explain the behavior of Jeremiah, who endured starving and exposure and a dung-filled dungeon because of his faith and love. The apex of the prophet's motivation was not self-realization, but the revelation of God's purpose. The categories from physical needs up to self-realization pale into insignificance when his love brings Jesus to the cross, or when the apostle Paul chooses hunger and exposure and beatings under the constraint of the love of Christ. The same point is made by the long line of witnesses presented in the eleventh chapter of Hebrews, or by the martyrs who have succeeded them in the continuing story of the church.

If, as we have maintained, the primary motivations in the church arise from faith and love—with a number of other factors supplemental—how does the leader's authority fit in?

WHY PEOPLE FOLLOW LEADERS

We began this chapter with the observation that authority is a kind of power. We saw that subjection to power creates resistance, yet the very nature of leadership involves the ability to see that persons act in certain ways. It was natural then to explore motivation: to see if we could discover why persons act in particular ways and what this would suggest to leaders.

With this information in the background, we now ask: Why do people follow leaders? Weber, the German sociologist, did helpful work in this area.[8] He observed that resistance to the exercise of power was lowered and people even developed enthusiasm for work on projects when they thought the leaders had a right to exercise power. He developed the proposition that authority is legitimated power, and saw that power could be legitimated by charisma, or by tradition, or by reason. Let us examine his three bases for legitimation in a Christian context.

Charisma

The sociologist's use of "charisma" may be confusing to Christians. He borrowed the concept from Paul but did not take the whole idea. "Charisma" for Weber is the quality in a leader which makes people want to follow him or her. This quality is difficult to identify and seems to differ as the needs and interests of constituents vary.

Appearance and size are sometimes important. Moses was a commanding figure. So were King Saul and

George Washington and Abraham Lincoln (though the latter was considered extremely homely). David, on the other hand, was not very large, and one gets the impression that the apostle Paul was small and not particularly attractive. A friend maintains that famous pulpits are usually filled by tall ministers, but he seems to have forgotten Harry Emerson Fosdick and Clarence Edward Macartney. Other attributes seem to be more important than the physical ones.

The psychological makeup of a charismatic leader appeals to constituents. They seem to identify with one who incarnates their needs, interests, attitudes, enthusiasms, or frustrations, or conveys the impression of capacity to be what they would like to be—and to help them achieve their goals. Such a person may draw out and focus subconscious drives by symbolic words and actions. Adolf Hitler and Winston Churchill both had this gift, as did John F. Kennedy and Martin Luther King, Jr. But note that in the Germany of the early thirties Kennedy would have received little attention from the frustrated masses waiting for a spark, and in the United States of the fifties Hitler would probably have ended his days as an unnoticed paperhanger.

A large church at the center of a great city once had a fine big charismatic pastor. He died after more than twenty years of splendid ministry there and was replaced by a little, vigorous man who proved to be even more charismatic than his predecessor. Membership and attendance grew despite deteriorating neighborhood conditions. Creative projects were undertaken in the community and the whole world. People came to see how it was done, and after ten years one group persuaded the minister to move to its church, which faced a comparable situation, with larger resources, in another city. But in ten years of heartbreaking work there, the minister was never able to recapture his charisma. He found it again when he moved to a third congregation. In the meanwhile, back at the first church his departure had been followed by a call to a tall, handsome, and spirited young man of undoubted gifts for ministry. Within three years of his installation he realized that the church was falling apart and accepted a call to a distant congregation, where he proved to be a highly charismatic leader. The first church tried again. It called an unimposing minister of middle age who led the congregation to a veritable resurrection of power.

One reason organizations learn to rely on other legitimations in addition to charisma is that it is most unpredictable. However, as we shall see, it is indispensable. If a church cannot have it in a pastor, and many cannot, it is all the more important to identify and involve in the life of the church charismatic members.

Charisma is not solely the possession of a particular leader, but rather the product of social chemistry developing between one and the many. It is more likely to emerge when a leader has certain qualities. One, as we have seen, is possession of empathy enriched by sensitive caring. Capacity for a rapid rate of energy discharge, which is often described as vitality, can be important. Hunger for accomplishment, related to a sense of destiny or of a divine call, may be determinative. Courage is always admired and frequently rallies followers, especially when it is demonstrated in decisiveness and refusal to accept defeat. Most of all, the faith discussed in the first chapter can make a person charismatic in Weber's sense—as well as in the New Testament sense.

Tradition

Contemporaries said of Jesus that he spoke with authority and not like the scribes. This is usually interpreted to mean that he simply stated a truth and let it stand, or put the force of his personality behind it—while the scribes felt they had to buttress their positions with quotations and precedents. But note that he spoke and acted in a tradition which gave his words and behavior meanings they could not have conveyed without the aid of the tradition. Dropped down on a different continent at a different time among people with a different past, he might not have been understood. The long development described in the Old Testament was God's careful preparation for what his son came to do.

The Christian leader today has the backing of a rich tradition which gives legitimacy to his or her use of power. The authority which results is often described as declarative. Jesus said to Peter, "I will give you the keys of the kingdom of heaven, and whatever you bind on earth shall be bound in heaven, and whatever you shall loose on earth shall be loosed in heaven" (Matt. 16:19). The words "bind" and "loose" mean "teach as true" and "teach as false." The gift is promised to the believing man or woman who recognizes Jesus as the Son of God and what he represents as the touchstone of truth about everything. This is underlined when Peter attempts to use his authority in a way out of harmony with the whole thrust of Jesus' life and ministry. He is immediately warned that far from exercising divinely approved authority, he has lost his legitimation and is talking like the devil. The thrust of the whole account is that a Christian leader may act authoritatively so long as the assumption is made that God's revelation of himself in Jesus Christ will provide the right answers.

Declarative authority is the right to proclaim in word and deed the good news revealed in the life and death and resurrection of Jesus Christ, and in the Bible which gives his context and explains the full meaning of the incarnation. The Word became flesh. This was the ultimate revelation. By its very nature as real flesh, the human body of the Son of God had to belong to a particular time and place. If everyone in the world is to know about this event, there must be witnesses to spread the information and explain its meaning.

The original witnesses were soon gone. Their testimony had to be identified, preserved, passed on, and interpreted in a changing and often hostile world. The church must be sure that the apostolic witness, insofar as possible, is uncontaminated by human misunderstanding and prejudices. The good news and its implications in each age must be translated into new languages and strange thought forms so that it is clearly understood.

The task is infinitely complex today. The universe of discourse is shaped by information and perspectives expressed in more books and periodicals than any ten persons could read in their lifetimes. The church has to understand the hidden assumptions or open propositions that place faith in jeopardy. It must deal with these as well as with the increasingly strident claims of rival religions and the more subtle blandishments of secular or pagan cults of pleasure or success or national aggrandizement. It is obliged to spell out the ethical implications of Christian faith with awareness of nearly two thousand years of hard thinking in a new context in which each issue—personal, social, vocational, economic, or political—has complicated ramifications. To these ends, it must have persons firmly rooted in the traditions and at home in the modern world.

A leader who speaks out of the Christian tradition has a legitimate authority in the church which we all recognize. Such authority may be exercised in the presentation of expositions of Scripture. These proclaim the good news, and by the power of the divine Spirit shape the thoughts and intentions of the fellowship. Further, they constitute a never-ending critique of all that is being done in response to the grace of God. The authority also has legitimacy when used in the development of services of worship, including the sacraments, in which the whole gospel shines like a many-faceted jewel. It functions properly in meetings and as people work together in mission, with the leader encouraging the use of the straightedge of God's revelation in Christ for setting a course or evaluating proposals and actions.

When a congregation issues a call to a pastor, it is arranging for a resident theologian—a servant of the Word of God in its midst. When the pastor exercises the declarative power inherent in this function, there should be no question of its legitimacy. The authority will be recognized as long as he or she speaks out of the tradition, or acts it out. The people have a right to expect solid knowledge of the Bible and church history and systematic thought about the gospel, as well as constantly developing powers of interpretation.

This theological task is, of course, not the exclusive

responsibility of the pastor. Everyone who accepts the divine invitation to join the family is expected to become an informed witness to the good news, a servant of the Word. Church officers have authority among such people if they shape the life of the congregation according to the biblical tradition. It will not be enough to ask questions of expediency. If the officers are to use power rightly, they must view all that they undertake in the light of the gospel. This applies to relationships, plans, programs, recruiting and training, buying and selling, use of buildings and equipment, and the securing and spending of resources. To take off in any direction without a theological compass and expect Christian people to follow is a betrayal of trust ultimately destructive of the legitimation that confers authority. The Christian leader's authority is declarative. It has a sound base within the Christian tradition and in no other setting.

Rationality

Weber's observations indicate that there is a third basis generally accepted for authority—namely, rationality. Certain activities are required if accepted objectives are to be achieved. Individuals can be found who will perform these functions if the group involved will accord them the right to exercise certain powers. The accomplishment of the purposes is worth the surrender of carefully designated freedoms of action. On this ground, arrangements are made for a hierarchical social structure in which responsibility and authority are distributed in the interest of effective corporate action. The natural resentment at being directed by someone is removed or much moderated by the shared desire for worthwhile goals.

The sociologist calls this "bureaucratic" legitimation because it involves the development of logically structured task groups or "bureaus." "Bureaucracy" has become an odious term because those working in these rationally constituted structures too often substitute for the original goals of the bureau their own benefits from the arrangement. They are tempted to value their authority not for its designed productivity but for the satisfactions it brings them. This subversion need not occur. To prevent it, leaders must never cease to keep before bureaucratic workers the overwhelming importance of the group purposes. In the church this means holding up in word and deed the mission that Christ has given his church, and the divine love which inspires our full devotion to his purposes.

Another problem faced by bureaucratic or rational structures is that of discipline. People working in such an arrangement are postponing some satisfactions in order to meet group goals. This calls for a high level of maturity or a willingness to submit to authority—which rational pressures alone cannot maintain. The result is that the bureaucratic institutions of business and industry, education, and government require a steady infusion of charismatic and traditional leaders. For these they owe a great debt to stable families and churches which provide support for rational behavior. The church itself is fortunate in having, as we have seen, powerful charismatic and traditional forces at work within it. This can take the curse off the bureaucracy which it needs because it has a mission to perform which benefits from rational arrangements.

From the very beginning, the church has experimented with rational structures for getting its work done. Its Lord appointed apostles and assigned responsibility and authority in the light of particular situations. As these men passed from the scene, Christians agreed on different structures and assortments of authority. Among Jewish Christians, they organized according to the synagogue pattern. Gentile Christians, to allay suspicions of Roman officials about their group meetings, probably used burial-society arrangements at first. Visiting witnesses and organizers and local officers emerged and were recognized as having defined authority. The view was that the risen Christ, by his Spirit, endowed members with gifts needed by the church and appointed them to serve. The church recognized the gifts and the need for them and the fact of the divine appointments. They marked the individuals for service in the required areas. Gradually they defined positions essential for the church's mission and clarified the endowments and training needed by one who was to perform effectively in a particular position.

The system is quite logical. The one who really knows what is needed is the Lord of the church. He guides the gathered faithful to decisions about the needs, the tasks to be performed to meet them, and the equipment that must be possessed by those who occupy strategic positions. Next, he endows members with the capacities required, and encourages their inclination to prepare and to serve. Finally, he enables the congregation to recognize the particular individuals he is calling to be pastors or officers, and to call them in his name.

Individuals who are aware of pressing needs in the

church and the world must consider whether Christ is calling them to leadership. We know from the experiences of others that the call may begin in vague stirrings of concern or a sudden conviction of obligation. It may be backed up with a sense of fitness or a feeling of inadequacy accompanied by a determination to acquire the needed attitudes, knowledge, and skills.

The individual is not the best judge of his or her ability to take leadership but must take seriously the view of the church. Hunger and thirst for office is not a sign of readiness, as Jesus reminded his disciples (Matt. 20:20–28; 23:1–12). On the other hand, a sense of unworthiness or inadequacy is not a sound basis for refusing a call to lead if a company of God's people believe they recognize in you the person whom Christ has chosen for a task.

The congregation's part is crucial. The people must define the needs in the light of the gospel. They must establish positions designed to meet the needs, to relate the positions to one another, and to distribute responsibility and authority which ensure effective coordination. They must recognize aptitude and competence and see that chosen leaders have the requisite faith, knowledge, and skill. In all of this, they have the assurance of guidance by the Spirit of their Lord, but they know he ordinarily works through the human intelligence and corporate wisdom he gives them. The authority that is given to leaders out of this process comes directly from Jesus Christ, the head of the church, through the Holy Spirit's work in the individual and corporate minds of the members. There can be no question of the legitimacy of this power.

THE AUTHORITY OF THE SERVANT

The nature of the authority in the church is defined by the Lord. Jesus deliberately turned his back on all the ideas of power held in the world and proposed something new: "servanthood." "Servant" and "slave" are strange words for leaders, but the early Christians took Jesus seriously. They remembered that he had come "not to be served but to serve" (Mark 10:42–45). Paul repeatedly calls himself "a slave of Jesus Christ," and we find this same description adopted by other New Testament writers (Rom. 1:1; Gal. 1:10; Phil. 1:1; cf. II Tim. 2:24; Titus 1:1; James 1:1; II Peter 1:1).

The ideal our Lord set forth was for all Christians. Whatever they did for their brothers and sisters in the family of God was to be a "service." Jesus used a word that has become familiar to us in its translation as "ministry." The image behind it is that of a person waiting on others at a dining table. Each Christian is to serve others in the spirit of Jesus, who clearly stated his intention: "Let the greatest among you become as the youngest, and the leader as one who serves [ministers]. For which is the greater, one who sits at table, or one who serves [ministers]? Is it not the one who sits at table? But I am among you as one who serves" (Luke 22:26ff.).

The church has found this to be an uncomfortable idea, and has rarely discovered individuals able to live up to it, or even to try. To many who take responsibility in the church it seems to violate the basic nature of leadership. How can one pull people together and move them into action without the trappings of power? The answer is that Jesus did. The towel is not ordinarily thought of as a tool of leadership, but in the hands of Jesus it was. The cross was the last place on earth anyone would look for a leader, but Jesus changed that.

Our Lord insists that faithfulness to his intention must be at the heart of all that a Christian does, and this includes the leadership functions. To the extent that self-glorification or self-aggrandizement or any other goal—however amiable—is part of the motivation of a leader, the assumption of responsibility falls short of leadership in the Christian sense; it is something less than service (ministry). This is not to suggest that a Christian (minister) should have a low opinion of self or service offered to God. It is, rather, to indicate that the value of an activity is to be weighed in terms of its faithfulness to the divine intention. This means that Christian leadership is to be developed and evaluated in the clear light of the gospel.

It also means that servanthood takes on dignity and power because it is God who is served. We feel this as we see Jesus in the upper room. "Knowing that the Father had given all things into his hands, . . . he . . . girded himself with a towel . . . and began to wash the disciples' feet" (John 13:3–5). How often that scene comes before our eyes as we face demands for humble service.

A woman whose son had been arrested in the night called a minister just as he was about to leave for a national board meeting. "I am beside myself with worry," she said. "Will you go with me to court this morning? Joe has been to the boys club at your church. He is not a bad boy. Maybe you can persuade the judge to give him another chance." The minister did just that, though it meant he had to miss the board meeting, where he was to preside. The action was typical. Incidents like this had established a ministerial authority that enabled him to shape a powerful congregation. Also, without a scramble for high office, it gave him great influence upon a whole denomination. He understood that the Christian leader is not asked to function without authority but rather to use the kind of power Jesus used when he laid aside his royal prerogatives and lived among us as a servant.

4

The Leader's Style

Style focuses on the way the leader functions. Matters of flair, vividness, charm, and an aura of excellence or excitement have been considered as a part of charisma. Here we are interested in orientation, attitudes, and strategies.

TASK OR PERSON ORIENTED?

A minister seeking the reason for dissatisfaction among those who worked under his leadership attended a seminar on administration. It began with a game in which the participants were divided into three competing teams. At the end of an hour of playing—during which the contestants became much committed to their conflicting goals—a management consultant asked the individuals to report what had happened and how they felt about it. Those on competing teams spoke with strong feeling about this minister's ruthlessness. When the turn of his teammates came, they were even more vehement. In the effort to win, he had made decisions for the group, ignored ideas of others, gone off on his own to negotiate, and made it impossible for the

41

group to develop any united strategy.

He was shocked at these reactions and launched into a long "sermon." The burden of the talk was that God wants results. It was illustrated by references to the patriarchs and Moses, kings and prophets, apostles and church leaders. Leaders who get things done do not worry all the time about the feelings of people around them. The Bible expects dedicated folk to be hardy and tough. The ministers at the seminar had been frank and he would be, too; they were suffering from the softness and self-consciousness which was ruining our age. When he stopped, there was a long silence. Then he stomped off to bed.

The next morning no reference was made to the game and its aftermath. Just before the luncheon recess, the minister asked for the floor. "I just wanted to say that I made a fool of myself last night. I came a long way here to find out why I was having staff trouble. It was pretty clear during the debriefing on that game, but I got so angry I didn't see it until this morning. All my life I've focused on tasks to the exclusion of persons."

For the other extreme, join me as I listen with a pastor to a tape recording of an official board meeting he has conducted. There are eleven members present. After a prayer and some pleasantries, the minutes of the last meeting are read and approved. This takes a long time as extensive comments by members are reported. I stop the recording and ask the minister why the minutes were not duplicated and distributed. This would have saved precious time. The reply is that the clerk went to a lot of trouble to write the minutes. He enjoys reading them and the members like to hear what they said. The same explanation is given for the reading of several long committee reports. The discussion of these never seems to get anywhere. A proposal to change the time of morning worship comes from a committee. They have consulted scores of persons and believe an earlier hour would help to hold younger couples who seem to be drifting away. Almost everyone has a kind word for the committee. However, as two members are still opposed, the recommendation is referred back for further study. I learn that this has occurred at two previous meetings. It is done amiably, with good feeling all around.

The same fate befalls plans for a more vigorous stewardship effort. These are proposed as an answer to a growing deficit. I ask the pastor why everyone avoids pressing for some action. He says they are all fond of the stewardship chairperson and do not want to hurt his feelings. The proposal reflects on what he is now doing. Further, if would be difficult for some members to increase their giving, though it is pointed out that the per capita is about half the denominational average.

The membership committee reports last. It wants to develop teams to visit inactive members and newcomers. Everyone has an opinion about whether this should be done and if so, how. The pastor sees to it that each member has more than one chance to speak. When the meeting adjourns rather late everyone goes home happy, but nothing has been done.

The pastor says this is a typical meeting. He and the board have proudly recorded it to show me, as I begin a consulting effort, that they have learned to care about each individual in the group. They have indeed! But they have become person oriented to the exclusion of task orientation. Each board member is getting satisfaction from participation but escaping the pressure to grow which comes from the necessity to do something. They are misusing human relations insights to avoid responsible action.

When we visit the church we find a country club atmosphere. Persons appear to be at the center of everything. This is appealing, until we realize that God is not at the center. What he wants is given second billing. His will is not merely that those near him are happy together. They are to lose themselves in serving him, and thus find themselves as they extend the family spirit to the ends of the earth. It is a misreading of the divine intention to act as if concern for persons eliminates responsibility for mission.

Increasingly in seminars we are uncovering this pattern. It was not always so. Some years ago a management consultant from the business world shook his head in amazement at the exclusive task orientation he found among a high percentage of ministers at three successive seminars. Both the percentage and the degree exceeded that which he found in businessmen and industrialists. Most of these men were pastors of large churches. Their ruthlessness toward persons who got in the way of corporate goals contrasted strangely with the attitudes of their Lord. Happily, the interest in interpersonal sensitivity has changed this dramatically in the last ten years. But indications are now that the shift has gone too far. Too often churches have an exclusive person orientation rather than a marriage of task and person.

What is involved in a balanced perspective? As we work through the processes by which leadership takes place, we will see that the effective practitioner must always keep in balance the group's goals and the needs of the individual members.[9] One or the other focus may dominate at any moment, but if the other perspective is not operative, leadership will be flawed. Style has to do with the way various components of leadership are exercised.

COMPONENTS OF STYLE

The fulfillment of a task or the achievement of a goal requires a strong sense of *responsibility* for the goal. This involves the ability to see the whole picture without fogging it with overmuch detail. It includes a habit of mind which breaks the task down into a manageable sequence of steps, and determined action which moves through them to the end. Because other persons are involved, the sense of responsibility is likely to be effective only if shared. The whole picture has to be communicated without distortion, and sharpened as others offer corrections and improvements. Others also need to have a part in the processes that move toward the goal so that their commitment will be more than formal.

Creativity is important in any group enterprise—and the church is no exception. The mission and values of the people of God are remarkably constant but if they are to be taken seriously, subsidiary objectives must be designed and undertaken in every generation. These will not be the product of persons content to manage things as they are. There must be innovation and new visions. A creative leader may therefore be a precious asset. But he or she will move the church toward its goals most effectively if others who have promise are identified, and with dogged patience involved in experiences that reveal and unfold their capacities.

Judgment—the ability to analyze a situation, to evaluate the quality of a piece of work or an individual's capacities or performance—is a priceless asset in the achievement of group tasks. The person is much needed who knows what information is required and how to find it; who is aware of costs, the limits of resources, and how to get what is needed; who is able to set priorities rather than dealing with all problems as if they held equal urgency. In the exercise of judgment, which is basically a task-oriented function, it is important that the activity be neither blunted by unwillingness to confront irresponsible or undisciplined persons nor become alienating because of insensitivity to the needs and feelings of others. On the other hand, no amount of attention to persons can, with impunity, be substituted for good judgment. If it is, the task will not be accomplished, nor will the needs of persons be met.

Decisiveness is another requirement for goal fulfillment. There must be willingness to choose—as over against delaying, postponing, and temporizing. As judgment calls for adequate information before action is taken, decisiveness insists that one act when one has all the information likely to be available within given time limits. It also calls for persons ready to start action when it is time to move. Any analysis of leadership performance should weigh resoluteness against dependency. There is a place for dependency. To rely on standard operating procedures for decisions that are often repeated saves time and energy. To follow the lead of a superior is usually wise. To depend upon an associate, a subordinate, or the working group to take the lead can make sense when the commitment of these persons and their growth may be nurtured in this way. This is often the case. Unfortunately, persons and groups that cannot make up their minds try to cover their insecurity and lack of courage from themselves and others by passing the buck. They can rationalize this behavior but cannot make it useful. The other side of the coin is the leader or the leadership group that precludes corporate decision-making by a regular practice of dictating premature decisions. We will look more closely at this problem in discussing strategies later in this chapter.

Perseverance is equally important in dealing with tasks and persons. Without determination, Moses would never have led the Children of Israel out of Egypt to the gateway of the Promised Land. Unflagging zeal like this animated the apostle Paul, enabled Luther to win an impossible struggle against church and empire, and in George Washington outlasted the endurance of those who opposed American independence. In each of these stories the outcome would have been tragic if the leadership had not persevered to the end. In each case the leader was as concerned about the persons involved and as patient with them as with the long-deferred goal. But the concern for the persons did not persuade Moses to encourage a return to Egypt's fleshpots. It did not induce Paul to encourage safety from persecution by a little legalism or judicious idolatry. It did not cause Luther to propose that churchmen hold on to comfortable livings by modest compromises, nor Washington to send men with bloody feet and empty stomachs home from Valley Forge. Each wanted for the people around him the fulfillment of the goal they held in common. They wanted also the growth and self-realization that would accrue as they kept on with the enterprise against all odds.

WAYS OF WORKING WITH OTHERS

The leader's style may be characterized by the strategies used in working with others. Much ink has been spilled in arguing the virtues of one way or another. In decision-making, the possibilities may be arranged on a line—with the leader deciding alone at one extreme (authoritative) and at the other extreme the leader depending entirely on others to make the decision (participative). In the other major responsibility of leadership communication the possibilities are more clearly presented in contrasting actions. We can see the possibilities in the following arrangements.[10]

Decision-Making Strategies

Authoritative

1. You decide, using information available.

2. You decide after getting necessary information from associates.

3. You decide after sharing the issue with associates as a group and getting their ideas and suggestions.

4. You decide after sharing the issue with associates as a group and agreeing on a decision.

5. You bargain with an individual or a group and agree on a decision.

4. You persuade an individual or a group to agree on a decision.

3. You become one of a group which together reaches a consensus or votes for a decision.

2. You serve as a facilitator.

1. You expect an individual or a group to make decisions.

Participative

Communicating Strategies

Authoritative ◄───────► *Participative*

1. You give clear and specific orders, explaining only what is necessary to the performance of the task.	1. You explain the issue and the basis for deciding to act in the prescribed way and ask the individual or group to follow this course of action.
2. You see that all communication among associates goes through you so that it will not be distorted.	2. You try to develop relationships and arrangements that will enable all participants to keep mutually informed about everything.

3. You accentuate the positive and discourage attention to weaknesses, mistakes, differences of opinion, and negative feelings.

3. You try to build mutual trust, encourage feedback and full consideration of positive and negative considerations.

There are legitimate and illegitimate reasons for using one or another of these strategies or their modifications in particular situations. It may be useful to examine some of these reasons.

Legitimate Bases for Authoritative Strategies

Time pressure is an important reason for using these strategies. A great deal of time is wasted in personal consultations, and particularly in meetings. This reduces working hours and often builds resentment. Some of the ablest church members become bored with interminable meetings dealing with decisions they feel could be delegated to individuals without serious loss of self-determination. Sometimes there is no time for consultation: an emergency calls for action or the issue will decide itself—and not necessarily well.

Specialized knowledge or expertise is widely accepted as a valid ground for more authoritative strategies. The goals for which the church exists or the processes to be used in reaching them may not be clear to a majority of those involved and a broad educational effort would take longer than anyone is prepared to wait for the decision. A pastor or a committee may have hard-won qualifications for interviewing and recommending an associate pastor or an organist. A theologically educated individual should be heard on changes in worship or church school curriculum. When the Scriptures and the experience of the church and the leading of the Holy Spirit all seem to an individual or a group to press in a particular direction, authoritative action is justified.

Expectations, informal or written into a job description, may call for authoritative strategies. Those who set up a position may make it plain that certain kinds of decision-making are part of the job requirement. Or it may be that a predecessor has set a style which cannot easily be changed.

Once in a four-day management game, the "death" of the authoritative old entrepreneur who built the business occurred on the morning of the third day and his son took over with all sorts of participative ideas. By noon the "management staff" were so upset—though it was a game—that few of them could eat lunch! A sudden shift from the authoritative to the participative is likely to give the impression that the leader does not know what he or she is doing, or is weak. This creates severe anxiety, and often hostility, and presents the would-be participative leader with an unhappy surprise. It may also make it difficult to move toward desirable strategies over a longer period by the careful educational approach required.

A comparable situation exists in churches where the majority of members are used to having other persons make decisions for them on the job, and tend to regard participative overtures as signs of weakness or laziness. And at the other extreme, in congregations largely composed of persons who must make important decisions day after day, there is a tendency to view with impatience requests for decisions in areas which they believe to be outside the spheres of their knowledge and expertise. They have used the good sense to insist on leadership that possesses these qualifications and, furthermore, has the leverage of the position they have established. An authoritative strategy is expected.

Implementation of corporate decisions sometimes requires a succession of smaller decisions which are in a sense contained in the choices already made and need only to be logically developed by a person of integrity and sound judgment.

Illegitimate Bases for Authoritative Strategies

The desire to dominate people turns the authoritative into the authoritarian. This ugly lust for an end to all limits upon one's freedom, satisfied by eliminating the freedom of everyone else, is the very epitome of sin. It strives to deify the leader. It is the exact opposite of Jesus' view of the leader as the servant of all. It is insidious and has the serpent for its symbol, because it is rarely noticed by the inflated tyrant until the swelling has disfigured underlying humanity. Long before its subject realizes what has happened, the objects of this lust have become aware of it and their alienation, however hidden, begins to work itself out in ways that will frustrate the authoritarian. God has not made the world a congenial place for petty deities.

A person who is trying to serve God in his church does not need to wait for events to mock arrogance. Rather, to be part of a Christian fellowship is to be exposed to the truth which can be spoken through other members. Those with authoritarian tendencies can often be helped by attending seminars designed to make them aware of their reasons for using particular strategies. The Holy Spirit guides Christians, but the evidence is rather overwhelming that to nip the lust for domination in the bud, he ordinarily uses social means in addition to solitary Bible-reading and prayer.

An overestimation of one's knowledge and expertise often lies behind the unwarranted choice of an authoritative strategy. The leader exhibits a disdain for the capacities of others and an impatience with their limitations which contrasts strangely with the picture of the Christian in I Corinthians 13. Such behavior frequently has its roots in a basic anxiety about one's own adequacy. The leader fears comparisons, and finds reassurance by flaunting certifications and experiences and scraps of information, or quietly goes ahead without any consultations. The result is an impoverishment of the church's life which could have been avoided had the leader troubled to discover the gifts available among the membership. The difficulty is that the blindness caused by one's overestimations of personal resources is the product of inferiority feelings which are hard to change. The Spirit may give one who recognizes these liabilities the capacity to rise above them in the assurance of importance in God's eyes, or he may work best through a trained counselor.

Legitimate Bases for Participative Strategies

The Holy Spirit speaks most clearly through the gathered church. The experience of Pentecost has set a pattern that inclines us to trust decisions reached by the body in councils and meetings. On this ground we believe we derived a dependable canon of Scripture and reach assurance about central doctrines. On this ground, all of Christendom comes to decisions about structures and leaders.

Information about persons or tasks may be available from others which is not otherwise available. Others may also be able to suggest what information is needed and where to get it. Under these circumstances, it would be foolish to "go it alone."

The gifts and expertise of a number of persons may be required. The Scriptures assure us that this is true in many situations confronting the church. The talents to be found in our churches bear this out.

The viewpoints of all involved will give a broader and clearer perspective. Self-interests and prejudices may be balanced and offset if all are heard on issues that affect them.

Commitment born of participation in decisions is important. This is particularly true at the present time when the culture of most members assures resistance to programs or activities chosen without their participation. The urgency becomes even greater when a major change may be involved or when members will be asked to furnish large resources.

The development of members as informed and effective workers and leaders may be a determining motivation for a participative approach to particular situations, since people learn and grow through involvement.

Limited power may make it impossible or imprudent to act without involving others.

Illegitimate Bases for Participative Strategies

To avoid responsibility and evade decisions are reasons for the use of participative strategies which no one will defend. The motivation is often hidden in the subconscious, but the user may uncover this subterfuge when he or she goes on to furnish excuses and point out scapegoats. What emerges under these circumstances has only the protective coloring of participative forms. It might better be called a "laissez-faire" strategy since, unlike the participative type of leader, this person really puts nothing of the self into the enterprise—or invests so little as to have no effect on the outcome. The result is a poor quality and quantity of work, and poor relationships and personal development among the people involved.

To make it easy and pleasant for people seems a good reason for participative strategies, but this motivation subtly changes the nature of the participation. It downgrades persons and the church of which they are a part by suggesting that their mission is less important than their comfort and pleasure.

The desire to be approved and liked is another unworthy motive for turning decisions over to others. Many church leaders grew up in families where the conduct of the children was socially controlled. While all people want to be approved and liked by those around them, people from such families are even more sensitive at this point. While strict social control is certainly better than the sadism inspired by physically brutal control of young children, it can result in too great a desire to please others. From time to time, it needs the balance of our Lord's assurance that blessedness may be connected with persecution.

It is obvious that competent leaders will use a mixture of strategies. The particular blend of the authoritative and the participative in a given situation will depend on the views and habits of the leader and the elements in the situation. However, in test circumstances where logical considerations definitely pointed toward a more participative approach roughly 75 percent of the participants used an authoritative strategy. When the authoritative stance was reasonable, close to 97 percent used it.[11] This suggests that there is a strong bias in most leaders toward an authoritative approach. The tendency is due, as we have seen, in part to the internal pressure of the leader's own needs and in part to a limited knowledge of processes that are used in a participative approach, which are discussed in the third part of this book.

MINICASES TEACH APPROPRIATE STYLES

It may be interesting and informative at this point to work in a group on some concrete material. The minicases with which this chapter ends briefly describe situations faced by pastors and lay leaders. Deal with as many as you can, acting in the indicated role. After you have decided how you would approach the situation, meet as a group to compare styles. Examine your intuitive and reasoned solutions in the light of material in this chapter.

In Dealing with These Situations You Are a Pastor

1. One of your associates has been performing inadequately for several months. You have talked with him or her several times. Each time you have received a promise of better performance, but you do not see any evidence of this. Before recommending dismissal, you are making one more attempt. He or she walks into your office and asks, "Did you want to see me?"

2. Attendance at Sunday school, which operates during morning worship, has built up until additional children cannot be accommodated. The solution that appeals to you is the institution of a second service of worship with accompanying Sunday school.

3. You are asked by a representative of the national church for the names of several members who could give a thousand dollars or more to a special mission fund. There are three families that could do this, but you know that the church must replace a roof this year and that a group of young adults in the church want very much to begin a migrant program that will cost an additional three thousand dollars a year.

4. The Reverend James Masterson is a member of the staff under your supervision. He is in your office and says, "I think I should be doing more preaching." You remember that his references indicated strengths in pastoral care but warned that he was a dull preacher. It was agreed when he came that he would concentrate on pastoral care, and preach, at most, four times a year. You never announce in advance that he is going to preach as attendance drops spectacularly if people know he is to be in the pulpit.

5. Anna Minerva, the choir director and organist, was permitted by the minister you succeed to choose the hymns for services. The hymns she has chosen for your first service are atrociously sentimental and not related to the sermon topic you sent ahead. When you suggest changes, she says the congregation does not know them and the choir has practiced the hymns she chose. In addition, she gives you a list of hymns and anthems selected for the next six weeks.

6. Dr. Arthur Meadows, president of a local college, is teaching the adult Bible class. A committee from the group waits on you to complain that he has abandoned the Bible for Transactional Analysis and they are sick of it.

7. The chairperson of the nominating committee is talking with you on the telephone. She names four possible nominees for one place on the official board. You know one to be an alcoholic. One is a brilliant lawyer who would be a real asset but is disliked by the chairperson. One is a tiresome gossip, and the fourth is a person who is capable but quarrelsome.

8. A dedicated leader in the congregation approaches you before morning worship. He asks that you announce a Sunday afternoon organizing meeting of a new chapter of the American Civil Liberties Union. You know that some members are opposed to this development on the grounds that "the ACLU has supported radical causes."

*In Dealing with These Situations You Are a Lay
Leader*

9. Individuals from a number of churches have held
a meeting in the interest of evangelism. No pastors
were present. They plan to invite a well-known evange-
list to conduct a series of services next year under lay
sponsorship. One of them calls you with an invitation to
join in the planning and sponsorship.

10. As chairperson of the Christian education committee, you are asked by Joe Larkin to renew his contract as a paid adviser to the senior high fellowship. A
college senior, he must reply to another job offer within
a week. He says: "I know these kids. They are rough and
could make a lot of trouble if not handled right. I've
kept drugs and liquor out of the church, and the building has been well treated. I admit I don't know much
about religion, but any of the kids will tell you they
enjoyed the fellowship last year and have a good opinion of the church."

11. The official board has just elected you chairperson
of the stewardship committee. Before the committee
has had time to meet, the pastor hands you a paper
outlining a new program for the year ahead. He says:
"I'm counting on you to put this across. I know you can
do it." There are features in the plan that do not appeal
to you.

12. You are chairperson of the Christian education
committee. One of your most enthusiastic teachers is
Sam Pyne. He is the outstanding member of a large
family. With in-laws and cousins, the Pynes account for
at least a quarter of the congregation on a Sunday morning. Sam's business requires travel but he always ar-

ranges to be at home on Sundays for his high school class. A distraught mother calls you to demand that Sam be removed from his teaching post. Her daughter reports that he has been making improper advances to several of the girls.

13. The new pastor is a dynamic person and everyone likes him. Unhappily, after the first few weeks the sermons have become moralistic and rambling and dull. You recognize that very little time is being spent on preparation.

14. The eighth-grade class has made two large, colorful, and somewhat crude banners. They ask you, as chairperson of the worship committee, to approve their plan to hang them at the front of the church.

15. As chairperson of the property committee, you are approached by the advisers of the senior high fellowship. They feel the group will function better if Sunday evening meetings are held in the church parlor. The bare basement where they now meet is all right for games but a poor setting for worship and business sessions. The women's association has just spent a large sum on a new rug and fine furniture.

16. Mark Stratford has left the church twenty thousand dollars. The official board is discussing use of the money. Some want it invested as endowment. Others propose a redecoration of the place of worship, "which hasn't been touched for years." Several are in favor of spending the money in one year on televising the service "so we can reach the unreached and build a larger constituency that will be a living endowment." Two younger members urge that half of it be given to the new welfare rights organization "which is trying to get justice for the kinds of people Jesus helped." As a long-

time board member, you are asked to suggest a course of action.

Your Own Cases

After dealing with these situations, your group may wish to write down in a few words just how you have dealt with some specific situations in your own church. What orientation was dominant? Were the strategies appropriate? To what extent did Christian convictions shape your actions?

5

The Church as an Organization

The apostle Paul suggests in several of his letters that the church is a continuation of the life of Jesus Christ on the earth. He speaks of it as "the body of Christ," and declares that each Christian is a "member" of this body. (I Cor. 12:12–27; cf. Rom. 12:5; II Cor. 10:17; Eph. 1: 22–23; 4:4–16; Col. 1:18, 24; 2:18–19; 3:14–15.) As the apostle sees it, when one becomes a Christian he or she is in a relation to Christ and other Christians similar to the relation of arms and legs, ears and eyes, and internal organs of a physical body to the head and to one another. The constituting relationship is love, but it goes beyond the family experience to something that may be described as organic.

MISSION REQUIRES ORGANIZATION

To be a Christian is to be a member. This is a radical new concept. The full thrust of it is lost in the modern world because so many groups have borrowed the term for a casual relationship among participants in a voluntary society. Paul has in mind a status and function much more fundamental. Members cannot be alive and functional without the head or without one another. Each member has a particular function which benefits all, and draws for sustenance upon all the others. Also the whole body reacts with its environment through the members.

The conception has much in common with the contemporary idea of the organization, which is conceived as a group of persons functioning together, like the organs of a body, in the interest of common goals that no one of the individuals could accomplish alone. Such units come into being whenever people work together. They develop social structures to facilitate the work, whether these are consciously designed or not. All of them, and in this the church is no exception, are characterized by specialization of function and the consequent need for leadership.

It is sometimes argued that since the church is brought into being by God's creative and redeeming acts and sustained by his Spirit, it is neither appropriate nor useful to deal with it as a human organization. The docetic heresy should make us wary of the assumption that when God is intimately involved humanity disappears! As a matter of fact, there seems to be ample New Testament warrant for treating the church as an organization.

The word for "church" in the New Testament means "a company of people called out." They are called out for a new relationship with God and with one another and to perform a mission. The company is described as the people of the new covenant because they carry forward the relationships and responsibilities of Israel under new conditions revealed and offered in Christ. (Jer. 3:31; Matt. 26:26–28; Heb. 8:1 to 10: 30; 12:22–24;

13:20–21.) This united people is referred to as "the fellowship" because they have a unique communion with God and with one another on the basis of Christ's life and death and resurrection, through the work of the Holy Spirit in their individual and corporate lives. (I Cor. 1:9; Eph. 3:8–10; I John 1:3–7.) This fellowship is called "the body of Christ," because each of the persons in it is related to the others as the members of the body are related, and the whole system of persons is directed and coordinated by Christ as the body is controlled by the head. Each of these images assumes that the church owes its life to an act of God: a call, an offer, a redemption, a quickening. But it also assumes that what comes into being is human—a company, a people, a fellowship, a body. If "the gates of hell," which is to say "the powers of death," will not prevail against the church (Matt. 16:18), it is not because it is removed by its behavior and relationships from the ordinary course of human events but because of God's intention for it.

If we summarize the meaning of the biblical images of the church, the picture that emerges is of a community of persons engaged in mission and functioning through a social structure.

The Persons Involved

The persons are responsible children of God called to live as members of his family. Every one of them is a sinner and keeps falling short of the divine intention. Since there are many persons, this means there is a great heap of sin in the church, and structures must take this into account. While God's grace causes him to treat proud and fractious men and women as his children, he only gradually entices them to behave them-selves. Part of this growth is furthered through life to-gether amid the rough discipline of the clash of wills. This means that organizations must be structured in such a way that the capacity of any individual or group to dominate a situation for selfish benefits or prejudiced ends is checked and balanced and subject to appeal, and that all members are subject to discipline.

However, sinfulness is not the deepest reality in human life. More fundamental are the God-given ca-pacities for freedom and responsibility and love, and individually unique endowments to be shared with the fellowship in mission. Adequate social structures will be open to the exercise of these gifts.

The Community

"To be reconciled to God is to become part of his reconciling community."[12] This involves a fellowship with Christ and one another, by his Spirit, through a common faith which arises in response to the divine love offered in Christ and is expressed in mission. Note that it is not social structures which hold the community together, but the common faith and love and mission inspired by his Spirit, and expressed with the aid of structures.

The community is characterized by love. There is love for God, expressed in prayer and praise and obedi-ence. There is love for one another, expressed in valu-ing each person for his or her uniqueness as well as for gifts and contributions. There is honesty and openness in an atmosphere of grace together with mutual sup-port and encouragement in growth. There is love for the world, expressed in mission. (I John 4:7–21; I Cor. 13:1–13; Eph. 4:15, 32; 5:1–2; Col. 3:13–15; John 3:16; Matt. 28:20; Rom. 1:14.)

The Mission

In every age the church has interpreted its mission as involving worship, mutual nurture, and witness through evangelism and social action. It has perceived that the nature of the mission calls for activities that are worldwide and at the same time designed to penetrate every aspect of human life.

When the church is functioning as God intends, it has a depth of penetration into every aspect of each member's life expected of no other agency. One can, for example, be part of an industrial enterprise by performing certain acts for a given number of hours each week. What you think about, or your beliefs, or how you treat your family, or what you do with the hours away from the job are matters of indifference to the company as long as you can perform well. Membership in the church is quite different: it is all-encompassing. Nothing about you is outside the church's concern. The whole person is involved in the relationships that make up the church's structures. This means that these structures are very complex and must bear more strains than any other human arrangements except those of the family.

The size of the church's task is to be measured not only by exploring the depth of its thrust into the lives of its members but even more by looking at its worldwide commission. Its Lord died for men and women everywhere, and his church is expected to make disciples of all people. It would be hard to overstate the

complexity of this task in the face of the current secular-
ism and pluralism and materialism and hedonism on the
one side, and fiercely competitive ideologies on the
other. Equally staggering is the Savior's expectation
that new relationships are to develop among human
beings as they are reconciled to God through his life and
death and resurrection. It is his intention that the
church shall serve this purpose. As the apostle writes,
"God . . . through Christ reconciled us to himself and
gave us the ministry of reconciliation" (II Cor. 5:18).
The church is, as one confession says, "to share this
labor of healing the enmities which separate human
beings from God, and from each other."[13] This means
involvement in the liberating struggles against the
dehumanization of technologies, the powerlessness of
the disfranchised, the victimization wrought by racism
and sexism, the obscenities of national selfishness that
create wars, the hunger stalking millions as a result of
their own heedless multiplication and of the selfishness
of others, the headlong pollution of the earth and waste
of its riches.

The scope of the church's mission makes it beyond
the capacity not only of individuals but of small primary
groups. A mission of the size committed to the church
can never be more than a dream without a network of
relationships for communication and coordination—in
short, an organization.

When a number of people are united in an important
purpose, and in its service attempt to overcome their
individual limitations by sharing responsibilities in a
continuing relationship, an organization comes into
being. A congregation is obviously such an organization, composed of persons doing together what no one

of them could do alone. It often has subgroups that function as organizations, while it is itself one among others in a much larger organization.

GROWING KNOWLEDGE ABOUT ORGANIZATION

To classify ecclesiastical units as organizations is more than a word game. It makes available a growing discipline which deals with the ways such units function and the processes by which they can more effectively fulfill their needs and carry out their purposes.

Knowledge about organizations has been building up over many years. Practitioners keep trying to find better ways of doing things and discuss problems with their peers. Observers describe what they see happening as people work together. Consultants take the fruits of experience from one place to another. Success and failure stimulate insight. Different specialists concentrate on particular activities and learn to offer useful advice in limited areas. Those who teach and write about organizations make generalizations and develop pictures of what is going on. They try to be descriptive in the hope that as patterns emerge it may be possible to estimate the probable effects of particular actions.[14]

The Classical School

In the longest reach of such effort the concentration is on getting things done and on the functions of those responsible. Attention is given to the development and maintenance of authority. There is interest in the design of formal structures (relationships). This involves organization charts and job descriptions. Exploration is made of the comparative values of centralization and diffusion of authority, and the number of other leaders one person or group can supervise. Other concerns include the use of time, accountability, decision-making, and delegation. Those with other primary interests frequently refer to this group as the Classical School.

They have much to offer the church. Their insights were extremely valuable as I worked over a two-year period with the Priests' Committee of the Catholic Diocese of Trenton to develop a basic job description for pastors. The instrument has great potential for improved relationships and better performance in the parishes of the fastest growing diocese in America. In one church a member of the official board persuaded his colleagues during an interview between pastors to reduce the number of their committees from thirty-two to eight. He knew that under ordinary circumstances coordinating the work of more than eight leaders or leadership groups makes the coordinator into a bottleneck. He did not share the surprise of other members when meeting times were reduced from four hours to two productive ones. In another instance, teaching a pastor how to delegate opened the way for him to be a much better administrator—and to spend more time on sermons which badly needed the extra attention. The concerns of the Classical School have relevance for us in the church.

The Human Relations School

This is also true of the preoccupations of those who have been termed by others, and sometimes by themselves, the Human Relations School. They give primary attention to persons, their needs and goals, rather than to group goals and executive functions. This emphasis emerges later than the Classical one as evidence piles up that the attitudes of the people involved have a great deal to do with outcomes. One would have to be blind not to see the implications of experiences like that at Hawthorne, New Jersey: women wiring switchboards are invited to make suggestions to expedite the work. They propose increasing the illumination. When this is done, more work is produced. Consulted further, they propose even more light on several successive occasions. Each time as illumination is brightened more work is done. Then the women conclude that the room is too bright. The glare is reduced and again the quality and quantity of work improves! As illumination is ultimately adjusted close to its original levels it becomes apparent that responsible participation is the key factor.

Following the implications of such cases attention is focused on persons. Subjects of particular interest are informal structures, motivation and styles of leadership, and communication. Meetings and small groups come in for a veritable explosion of concern. Group dynamics emerges as a discipline.

The church owes much to those who work in the human relations areas. The board of St. Andrews is helped to see that increasing the number of members participating in decision-making will enlarge the pool of those ready to serve. The minister of Berachah Church discovers how much is going on in meetings and what this knowledge can mean in more fruitful gatherings and better pastoral care. A group of senior pastors with staff problems begin to understand how to blend styles and develop capacities for consultative supervision.

The Structuralist School

Most recently those who reflect and write about organizations have recognized that the insights of both Classical and Human Relations Schools are essential, and that their value is greatly increased when they are brought together in a bifocal approach. All organizations exist for both group goals and individual satisfaction. The tendency of the Classical School to stress task orientation needs to be balanced with the Human Relations emphasis on persons. It is not either-or. Further, as attention is focused on relationships new insights emerge. An organization is seen to be a unity that is more than the sum of its parts. The relationships within it are perceived to be far more complex than appeared at first. Also, its transactions with its environment are recognized as more reciprocal than earlier observers noticed. Light is thrown on planning and change processes and on conflict. These interests are pursued in many places and with a variety of emphases. For convenience, and recognizing that some will reject the designation, we will follow one of the most distinguished among them in referring to this as the Structuralist School. The term is chosen because their attention is directed primarily to relationships that may also be conceived as social structures.

This school also brings rich gifts to the church. The emphasis on wholeness makes it plain that individual problems cannot be dealt with in isolation. Pilgrim

Church ignored this in putting on a drive to reactivate members who had ceased to participate. Twenty teams called on two hundred persons. Seven people returned to active membership, but three of the callers quit the church! All the attention had been directed to the inactives. The visitors had inadequate theological preparation and no report meetings where they could find understanding and support.

The recognition of complexity could save Second Church from disaster. In an effort to meet a budget crunch, the board votes to close weekday programs that serve community children and youth. Their families show no interest in the church and do not support it financially. Almost at once neighborhood conditions deteriorate. Windows have to be boarded up. The neighborhood begins to look run-down and dangerous at night. Attendance at evening meetings falls off. Dedicated members who found meaning for their lives in working with deprived children and young people seek places of usefulness elsewhere. Lacking exposure to Structuralist concerns, the board fails to recognize until too late that in a complex organization such as a church, cause-and-effect relationships are not simple.

Among the most fruitful observations of this school are those which have to do with the organization's environment. The board of Old First Church always recognized the importance of its surroundings. The members did what they could to keep up the neighborhood and even bought one property to keep it from becoming an eyesore. They fought against repeal of Sabbath laws on doctrinal grounds, but they also knew open stores would compete with services. They appreciated the value to the institution when newcomers found themselves seated behind the university president and across from the board chairman of the local bank. They believed sincerely that First Church was building moral character into the life of the city. They thought their substantial investment in world mission was helping to bring peace on earth and goodwill among all people. Now the friendliness of the environment and the church's impact upon it seem less certain. The redevelopment of proud old streets is at first threatening as the great family houses are replaced with high rise apartments. Then there is hope that the young couples moving in will bring new life. Unfortunately some of the ablest among them prove to be nomads. Within two or three years the breadwinners are promoted and they move on to another city.

Old First's personnel policies were devised for a more settled population. So were their methods of assimilation into groups. No one thinks of changing them. Nor is any serious thought given to weekday services or house churches when increasing numbers of members buy weekend cottages for summer and winter sports. The board enthusiastically supports government purchase of a nearby section of dilapidated houses for a state office complex. Too late they see that weekday parking is becoming next to impossible and at night the huge empty structures and plazas invite muggings. Luncheon Bible classes and a drop-in center to compete with local bars and offer friendship and counseling never come up for discussion. Seven hundred families move into a low-cost housing project within four blocks of the church. Efforts are made to welcome the newcomers, but "they are not our kinds of people" and few return after an initial visit. A member of the board is indicted for vote fraud. The son of another is jailed for selling drugs. One of the couples groups seems to be going all out for the new sex morality. The grandchildren of some of the members prefer to stay home from church to watch Sunday morning television programs.

This board is becoming painfully aware that the mission of the church cannot be performed in isolation. It has a part in a much larger network of relationships and must give attention to these. The church shares this predicament with all the other organizations around it, political, legal, educational, and so on. No wonder those interested in organizations are especially emphasizing their dependence on the environment and the ways they may influence it.

Organization Development

It is not surprising either that recognition of inter-relatedness within and without leads to a greater concern for planning and education. Planning is seized upon as the primary method by which the organization's purpose may shape its interior and exterior relationships and connected activities. Education is valued because it may help members to understand their situation and discover useful processes for meeting their goals. A number who share these interests see themselves primarily as consultants devoted to involving leaders in planning and change processes and educational experiences. They describe themselves as engaged in "organization development."[15] This discipline has evolved a literature but its proponents generally talk the same language as the Structuralist School.

The boards of Pilgrim, Second, and Old First

churches can arrange for a consultant to meet with them. He or she will help them to understand their situation and the processes available as they try to carry forward their mission, or they may learn to do this for themselves.

Science or History?

We now see that the study of organizations has followed three main lines of inquiry. The three have developed in sequence, with the latter borrowing freely from the former, but they go on side by side performing useful functions.

Note that each school perceives certain problems and develops ways of looking at them which suggest fruitful approaches. Some ecclesiastical writers to the contrary notwithstanding, current representatives of the schools generally lack interest in overall theories of organization which may be evaluated in behavioral and theological terms.[16] Their aims are more modest and attainable. Some researchers and consultants do speak of applying the results of social science as they recommend certain practices. They do in particular areas follow descriptive efforts with attempts to explain and predict.

The caution of J. Douglas Brown[17] is pertinent at this point, lest one give the impression that organizational behavior can be scientifically determined or predicted. He points out that each organization continues at all times to be subject to the complex and unpredictable initiations and responses of the individual human beings who make it up. "A thousand individuals reacting to a single stimulus, diversely interpreted, react on each other to create a system of responses which make logical analogies from physical science both ridiculous and dangerously misleading. Statistical analyses based on the proposition that although individual actions may be unpredictable, those of a large number can be predicted, overlook the fact that people are not molecules. The unpredictability of one person's response carries over to the unpredictability of a large number of people whenever freedom of action or thought exists. It is possible and frequently profitable to make generalizations about the ways individuals and groups behave in particular circumstances, but these are historical observations useful to the wise and intuitive rather than scientific laws."

Models

Human freedom may impair the calculus of probability on which theories depend, but there is another device which enables us to approach a subject with understanding—namely, the model. The model is an abstraction like a theory but it does not pretend to go beyond description. By judicious concentration on essentials, a model may help us to grasp the shape of an organization and what is going on in and around it. Of course, the history of models warns us that designers frequently leave out something later discovered to be decisive, but there is no escaping some risks.

Frequently a model is based on an analogy. The simplest currently applied to organizations is that of a network. Another is the ancient model produced by the apostle Paul for the church, that of the body with its organs. The very name assumes this model: it is an "organ-ization." How aptly this analogy pictures the most recent insights of the Structuralists about the organization's wholeness and inner complexity and interdependence with its environment. One might say this useful knowledge was there all the time in the Scriptures waiting for us to see its importance.

Systems Thinking

The most popular model at the moment is the system.[18] The word comes from the Greek term for "standing together." It is used for a complex unity of parts interacting with one another and with the whole, individually and as subgroupings. "Social system" has long been a synonym for "organization." It represents a somewhat higher level of abstraction than the body, which is seen to be a system. This model encourages us to see the organization of which we are parts in a sequence of larger and smaller social systems, some composed of a number of the others, but each maintaining an integrity so that it is more than the sum of its systems. Each also relates to systems it touches which may or may not be parts with it of a larger system. This model has been particularly useful in developing and now in communicating the major insights of the Structuralist School. Its activity is frequently referred to as "systems thinking."

Aspects of this model may be reduced to a diagram not unlike the organization chart of the Classical School. The crucial difference is that it shows the interdependence within and includes the environment in the picture. One danger of systems thinking appears in some of its diagrams which seem to have engineering antecedents and use terms like "input" for things as various as persons and ideas and money and heating oil. One virtue also comes from the mechanical analogy: we are encouraged to think about the extent to which "feedback" from elements in the environment can or should shape the organization and its activity. If the board of Second Church had engaged in a little systems thinking, they might have asked important questions about the kind of feedback they could expect from underprivileged youth excluded from programs in the building.

Summary

It does appear that theological considerations indicate it is appropriate and experimental results show it is useful to deal with the church as an organization. It also is clear that extensive efforts have produced a volume of knowledge about organizations which leaders may profitably explore and use. Let us now look further at some of this material.

THE NATURE OF ORGANIZATIONS

An organization is a social system that overcomes individual limitations, liberating and mobilizing energies for group goals and individual satisfactions, characterized by specialization of function, established relationships (structures), essential processes, and traditions.

Organizations come into being to overcome individual limitation. Together we can do things no one of us could do alone. Our association gives us a combined strength far beyond the attainment of any individual, and this mobilization of energy frees us from constraints otherwise inescapable and opens the way for remarkable achievements.

Group Goals and Individual Satisfactions

The ends for which people work together vary greatly, but there are always two sorts—group goals and individual satisfactions. The group goals of the church have already become apparent: worship, nurture, and witness. The individual satisfactions, in addition to meeting the mutual goals, may include joy in Christian fellowship or just in having friends, satisfaction in doing the will of Christ, opportunity for growth, and support in faith and in ethical behavior, as well as some less ideal benefactions such as a sense of importance unavailable elsewhere, acceptance in certain circles, useful contacts, and help in adversity.

So powerful are the individual satisfactions that they can easily come to be valued more highly than the mutual goals for which the organization was established. We have all seen this goal displacement taking place as congregations or their subgroups lose their dedication to mission and become country clubs or mutual benefit societies, or once-committed leaders develop more interest in a paycheck than in the church's purposes. There is nothing at all wrong with finding satisfactions in organized activity; indeed, the fact that it occurs strengthens incentive for participation in the organization, but there is bound to be some tension between the goals of the group and those of members for themselves. The wise administrator will be interested in maintaining a healthy balance.

Since organizations come into being for group purposes and are valued as they meet individual needs as well, they are likely to continue only as long as at least one of these two classes of incentives remains. It is ordinarily possible to change the goals of a social system without disaster if the individual satisfactions are maintained. Thus, a leader may shift the major thrust of a congregation's mission if the individuals and families are receiving valued pastoral care. An attempt to change at one time the organizational goals perceived by the members and the satisfactions available to them as individuals is a quick method of dissolution. Church leaders dissatisfied with a congregation's major goals, as well as with what it is doing for its members, will be well advised to work on these areas one at a time.

There is, of course, no escape from the consideration of new departures. Goals must be constantly reexamined as changing environments tend to make their forms obsolete and dissipate their motive power.

The Importance of Tradition

Few pastors or church officers are unacquainted with the importance and difficulty of change. But it is possible to miss the strategic value of tradition when this extends beyond the basic Christian inheritance and stamps a particular congregation with certain characteristics.

A church, like other organizations, develops within a tradition that is "an evolving, pervasive system of assumptions, habits of mind, customary behavior, and attitudes."[19] This tradition was shaped by leaders in the past as they dealt with conditions inside and outside the organization. As the conditions change, new leadership may reinforce, reinterpret, or change the tradition. They can never afford to forget the hold upon the common mind of the members of the things generally believed about the group's past and its implications. Before it is very old, a body of people develops a momentum. Sudden turns risk disaster. Stopping and then starting in a new direction uses up a great deal more time and energy than focusing on elements in the tradition which are allies of biblical imperatives or of responses to new needs. Thus, a congregation that has become a self-centered mutual benefit society may awaken to its evangelistic obligations when the missionary zeal of its founders and first members is vividly recalled in sermons and articles and drama. A church that has been building itself but neglecting its community may begin to show more of the compassion of its Lord when reminded of the tradition he started and how it was carried forward by earlier members of the congregation.

Strategy in the Light of Imperfections

A whole set of problems faced in organizational activity arises from the chronic imperfection of social systems. After all, as we have seen, they are made up of human beings who are far from perfect, and who have gifts very unevenly distributed among them—and often relate to one another as if they had been made in different shops. Their resources are always limited, and these are rarely distributed appropriately. The situation calls for careful analysis of the strategic factors in the particular system, and a refusal to be discouraged because perfection is out of reach. After all, as Etzione remarks, organizations—like light bulbs—are less efficient than we would prefer but they can do something very important. Of course, it is essential to apply electric current at the right point if the light bulb is to fulfill its destiny, and it is equally essential that energy be directed to the strategic place in an organization. How often we observe a pastor or church officer fretting about unattainable perfection, or working night and day at a project that could have come to fruition in response to a much more limited effort informed by some knowledge of the system and its field of forces.

A CHALLENGE TO LEADERS

The "force field" is shaped by the fact that every organization is characterized by specialization of function. This is essential when a group of any size works on a united project. To demonstrate it, we sometimes ask two groups of twelve or more each to build two towers of construction paper, each in a different room. The exercise is cast in the form of a competition with a strict time limit and three criteria for the better tower: height, stability, and aesthetic appeal. A limited amount of material is available on a table, to be divided by negotiation between the two groups. It quickly becomes apparent that the groups will have to arrange for specialization: negotiators, designers, cutters, pasters, assemblers, coordinators. The team that fails to act in this way at the outset usually fails to win.

Every working group finds it essential to establish at least two types of functions: working and leading. The *leading* function is primarily that of coordinating through keeping communication open, making required decisions, and motivating. In tiny primary groups everyone may share in the work and the leadership, but as the number of members increases and the task becomes complex, the functions must be assigned to individuals or small groups.

In the early church there were apostles, prophets, and teachers, and others described as "helpers," "pilots," "rulers," and those "over you in the Lord." As time went on, and especially when the apostles were no longer available, the congregations looked more and more for all the leadership functions to local fellow members; and we hear of elders and bishops (overseers), deacons (servants), and pastors (literally, "shepherds," which is also the derivation of "bishop," and focuses on the leadership task). (Acts 14:23; 20:17, 28; I Cor. 12:28; Eph. 4:11; I Tim. 3:1–2, 8, 10, 12; 5:17; Titus 1:7; James 5:14.) The basic function is that of service to the body of Christ in order that it may perform its mission in the world. Persons so engaged are the nerves and connecting tissues of the body, the servants of the servants of God.

Among those called to be his servants and servants of his people, God asks certain individuals in every generation to be leaders in the church so that the witness to the kingdom, which is a family, may go on and on to the end. Those who have begun to live in faith and hope and love may experience and share something of the kingdom's reality as they join in common worship and mutual nurture, and reach out in care and concern to the whole world.

How the leaders are to do this is the subject of the rest of this book. The processes involved will be explored in successive chapters.

BEYOND THE CONGREGATION

Before we turn to explore these processes, it may be useful to look beyond the congregation to the networks of communication and decision that have grown up to facilitate the church's mission in districts, regions, and nations, and across the world. These structures are obviously essential to the mission. They perform functions that are beyond the potentiality of the strongest congregation. Resources of personnel and money are carried from congregations to points of need in accordance with strategies cooperatively devised. Specialists are maintained to meet challenges to the faith by systematic thought about biblical implications for new circumstances. Gatherings are held to reach consensus about questions of faith and practice. Arrangements are developed for preparing ministers of the Word, meeting their special needs, and making them available to congregations. Programs are made to undergird the worship and mutual nurture and mission of specific churches, and to meet needs in areas beyond the competence of one congregation. Constitutional provisions safeguard the rights of individuals and groups, and provide for discipline. Our Lord's worldwide mission could not be implemented without these structures.

Those who work "behind the lines" in these tasks have unique opportunities for Christian leadership. While each responsibility may call for particular gifts and often special preparation, the qualities and processes we are discussing are of crucial importance in their work.

While our primary focus is on leadership in the local

church, and we maintain that its importance is second to none, we cannot forget the insight of systems thinking about organizations. It holds that in any social system it is utterly impossible to develop a simple cause-and-effect relationship between particular components since each member or system of members has both a cause relationship and an effect relationship with every other member and system of members, as well as with the system as a whole. This underlines the apostle's point that no member of the body can say to any other member, "I have no need of you" (I Cor. 12:21). It also suggests that leadership may be equally crucial at any point in the system—with only God aware of the most strategic place at any moment in time. Special honor for one position or another is as foolish as Paul makes it seem. Whatever its location, each leadership position in the church has unlimited potential and each leader needs the qualities we have discussed—and a mastery of the processes we are about to explore in order to involve the people of God in fulfilling his intentions.

6

Leaders as Coordinators

Organizing is a process going on all the time in any social system, including the church. It involves, among other things, developing in the minds of the members a picture of the group's life together, securing their acceptance of this model, and keeping it up to date. The model may have its tangibility primarily in the words and deeds of leaders and members. It may be embodied in a written statement, such as a constitution or bylaws, or have graphic form in an organization chart. It is useful because it defines the situation, suggests what particular members should do and expect others to do, and clarifies relationships.

THE ORDERING FUNCTION

The organizing function has been called the "ordering" of the life of the church, using a term that originally referred to setting troops in array for battle. How the church is to order its life for mission must be settled in each generation under the guidance of the Holy Spirit. Despite frequent insistence to the contrary, the church has regularly acted on the assumption that our

Lord, in the days of his flesh, offered no detailed answers to these questions—and expects his people to find
their way by reflection and experimentation in the light
of the gospel. In each period of its life, the church has
adopted social structures in general use and has ben-
efited from and contributed to criticisms and improvements of these forms and processes. We are all invited
to continue this enterprise.

The established relationships among people that
serve as frames of a social system are often called "structures," as though they were iron or wood frames of a
bridge or building. This is not as farfetched as it may
seem, for these connections between persons and
groups carry the weight of the group enterprise.

Formal Structures

Formal structures arise when specializations and authority relationships are spelled out and the procedures
for assignment to particular functions are established.
While a great deal of time can be wasted on refinements
of constitutions, bylaws, and organization charts, the
development of adequate documents can be very useful. Everyone benefits when there are clear statements
about the rights and privileges of members, the duties
and powers of officers, and the access to these roles, as
well as procedures for discipline and appeals. Written
law is a safeguard of freedom and a guardian against
goal subversion. Charts enable a group to weigh the
logic of relationships projected or in use.

A church officer in an administration class had an
assignment to develop an organization chart of his
home church. When he brought the result to the class,

he began by saying he now understood the ineffective-ness and petty conflict that had characterized the church for years. The arrangements assured that lead-ers would be engaged in duplication of effort, that boards and committees with fuzzy assignments would build resentments, and that persons of ability would shun office. When things are put down in black and white, there is opportunity to relate faith and structure, to design arrangements that relate persons on the basis of all we know about how human beings can function together, and to devise and deliberately effect changes in structures.

The Representative Principle

We know that people are more willing to give of themselves and their resources if they feel they have a part in decisions about the use of time and resources. In large groups it is not possible to have the intimate give-and-take that can produce consensus. A breakthrough toward the solution of this problem is the representa-tive principle. Individuals are chosen to represent large numbers of persons in deliberative groups or adminis-trative committees or task forces. One question that designers of representative structures must ask is how to keep the representative group small enough so that each participant can make an impact on consensus, while at the same time having enough representatives so that the people feel represented. Most churches seem to feel that there should be at least one official board member for every fifty active members. In very large churches this can mean that the board is so large it must do virtually all its work in representative committees. If there is a climate of trust, this may be entirely satisfactory. Difficulties with the representative system more frequently arise at the denominational and interdenominational level when members are separated from the actual decision-making by three to five layers of representation. These layers filter out communication and interest, as layers of insulation stop sound. The representative system is certainly the best procedure so far devised for assuring all a part in decision-making. It may be possible to secure more acceptance of the arrangement by more effective communication. In the situations where more than two levels of representation have developed, the solution may be more direct elections which eliminate one or two layers.

Too Much Structure?

Sometimes a church develops more structures than it needs to perform its mission. Often this is due to the continuance of organizations and committees after their goals have been met or are no longer relevant. Sometimes the situation arises because a congregation copies the organization chart of another church without examining the structures. There is a growing inclination among church boards to set up task forces, which differ from committees in being authorized to exist only up to a date set for the completion of a task. Such arrangements are suitable only for certain assignments. Responsibilities that must be discharged perennially would seem to be better served by committees that can develop members with valuable knowledge and skill and arrange for some continuity by integrating a few new persons each year. Committees are occasionally oversized in the interest of wider representation, but if they get beyond twelve members, the intention is foiled by the inactivity of some—or the committee's purpose is thwarted because it takes too much talk to get action.

Informal Structures

Informal structures come into being when formal structures have not been made or in situations where contractual arrangements seem to some members inadequate. Thus, a congregation elects an official board to give leadership, but if what they do is unsatisfactory to some members, informal pressure groups develop and often effect change in policy. If a meeting is conducted in such a way that some members feel they were not heard or were treated unfairly, an "after-meeting" is likely to redo the business around a coffee table. If a church neglects some aspect of the Christian's life or obligations, little groups often emerge with special interests.

The human relations school of organization theorists discovered that in industry the informal structures often had more to do with what happened in a factory than the official chain of command. An experienced and respected worker often sets the production levels more effectively than management. A highly regarded church member may exert more influence off of the official board than as a member of the board. A dictatorial pastor may establish control of the formal apparatus only to discover that the real power in the church is wielded outside the regular channels. These possibilities can be healthy. In some instances, the existence of informal groups calls attention to neglected persons or areas that may be cared for by an improved formal structure or by the enlistment of particular persons. It may lead to a policy of encouraging persons with special concerns related to the church's mission in developing new structures. It may supplement or strengthen the formal system. For example, this may occur when senior members, no longer in visible structures, are encouraged to express their ideas and extend support.

THE COMMUNICATING FUNCTION

Communication is essential to effective organizational activity because the achievement of group purposes is dependent upon dividing the required tasks among the members. Good communication makes options clear and opens the way for wise choices by individuals and groups. It clarifies the relation of actions to the desired results and increases motivation. It makes coordination easier through developing awareness of the actions of others.

A leader often has a message for another person or group of persons. (1) It may be information: "There will be a meeting of the official board on Tuesday at 7:30 P.M." (2) It may be a feeling: "It is very important to me that you attend the official board meeting Tuesday." (3) It may be an attitude: "I intend to do what I can to assure that our facilities are available to the new coalition on prison reform." (4) It may be a proposition: "You ought to speak up at the official board meeting."

Usually, a message will be recognized by the sender to have several of these elements. Unfortunately, it may have elements the sender does not notice. A feeling like love or pity or anger or frustration or suspicion may act as a filter to limit information or distort it. On the other hand, the sheer difficulty of packaging information about a situation or project may result in the package containing no hint of the feeling that could give it impact. It is therefore important that the sender develop the art of message-making, including clarification.

Once the message is clear to the sender, it must be *encoded* for transmission. Communication is rule-governed behavior. That is, ideas and feelings and attitudes are more likely to be understood if they are arranged in forms that have wide usage and can thus be recognized. This is obviously true of the basic convention of communication: language. A failure to observe the rules of syntax leads to confusion. Less obvious, but almost as important, is the choice of forms in general cultural use: a statement, a question, an order, a story.

The encoding process depends for success on a common set of rules known to sender and receiver. Vatican councils are becoming more difficult because more and more bishops are ignorant of Latin. The same kind of problem may exist for a native of Brooklyn in Appalachia, or a suburbanite in a ghetto, or a product of graduate education dealing with people who look just like his classmates but think and talk in other patterns. The receiver's experience and the mental framework built up to deal with it over the years will have a decisive effect upon what is received. A camera loaded with black and white film cannot receive color. My son is a bird watcher and when we walk in the woods together, he will hear and see a dozen species of feathered beauties which I miss completely. One of the communicator's tasks is to discover enough about the receiver's

past and current experience and related mental categories to make connections. My son can name a kind of
tree I know and suggest watching it for a flash of familiar color. Timing is, of course, important. If he knows I
am preoccupied with writing a chapter of this book, he
will wait for a more likely occasion to open my eyes.
The case is not so different when I am trying to help a
board make a decision on theological as well as utilitarian grounds. The mental computers of most of the
group may not as yet have the needed theological categories. I must begin by making contact with some of
their meaningful Christian experiences and ideas.

Once encoding is completed, the sender chooses
media or channels to get the message over to the receiver.

Marshall McLuhan has made many of us conscious of
the importance of media.[20] He divides them into "hot"
media, sharply defined and calling for little effort on the
part of the receiver, and "cool" media, which are designed to call out maximum effort on the part of the
receiver. The analogies of "hot" and "cool" are based
on the fact that a cold object "draws" heat from us. He
sees audio-aural and electronic-holistic media as "cool"
and visual-literal media as "hot." The implications of
these characterizations for the church are extensive.
For our immediate purpose it is perhaps sufficient to
observe that where information is wanted, the "hot"
media may prove superior in effecting both conveyance
and retention, while the "cool" media have the advantage when feelings and behavior modification are
desired.

Media used in church communications include (1)
spoken words to individuals (face-to-face, visits, tele-

phone) and to groups (addresses, sermons, discussions);
(2) *written words* (letters, memos, newsletters, bulletins, books, magazines, advertising); (3) *nonverbal expressions* (voice tone, facial expression, gestures, pos-
tures, settings, structures); (4) *holistic media* (movies,
television). Each of these kinds of media is affected by
the situation in which it is used, and the other persons
who have a part in the process. For example, a statement to another individual may have a different import
as it is offered in a private meeting, or before witnesses,
or on a telephone. A letter says quite different things if
it is handwritten or typed, duplicated or individually
addressed, or included in a newsletter or bulletin.

The receiver's attitude toward the sender affects reception. Response depends to a marked degree upon
the receiver's opinion of the sender's integrity, and the
relationship between them (caring or indifferent, trusting or suspicious). An impression of hypocrisy or self-
seeking or hostility blocks reception, as noise interferes
with hearing of sound. Paul in writing his first letter to
the Corinthians was concerned that attitudes and behavior of members were creating so much noise that
the gospel could not be heard.

Feedback is important. In models based on systems
thinking, it is usually pictured as a loop. This is like the
thermostat line on a heater, bringing back information
about effects. Such information is useful as we plan further action. Most of us rely on intuitive perceptions to
measure the effect of our efforts, and these are often
reasonably accurate. However, extensive research suggests that without deliberate and well-designed processes for securing feedback, the best communicators
are likely to be wrong about effects.

The church has some well-established ways of securing feedback. Quantitative information may be significant, though it must be weighed in the light of theological goals and environmental conditions. It is not difficult to keep and compare statistics on attendance, giving, membership trends, participation in activities, dependence on pastoral services, and use of facilities. Qualitative data come in as callers are sensitive and those visited are encouraged to be open. The data emerge in discussion and behavior at meetings. They flow back through personal contacts in the community and public expressions about the church.

Feedback may be encouraged by formal arrangements. Some pastors who meet every month have each agreed to establish a sermon feedback group of seven or eight persons. The same individuals serve for about six weeks and then are replaced by others. The group meets for a half hour after the Sunday service to discuss the sermon. The pastor is not present but agrees to listen to a tape recording of their discussion. A framework of reasonably nonthreatening questions is used: "Why do you think the pastor chose this text and topic?" "What did he say?" "Was it worthwhile?" "Were there points hard to understand?" "Was anything left out?" "Are there subjects you wish could be discussed in a sermon?" The answers throw surprising light on what is heard and what is not. There has been a notable improvement in the preaching of pastors who have taken this feedback seriously.

A board may design program questionnaires to be mailed or presented during visitations in homes or at organization meetings or in gatherings after a service. A letter of inquiry may be sent to prominent members of the community or randomly chosen neighbors of the church. Members may be induced to raise a succession of questions with those about them at work or play. In these instances the questions are carefully designed in connection with a full planning process of the sort described in the next chapter.

Whatever the method, feedback will be effective only if the congregation's leadership develops a plan for coordinating responses and acting on their implications, in the light of their faith.

The facilitation of communication is a major task of the leader. Relationships, meetings, and procedures must be developed in which participants have a reasonable chance of hearing and understanding and responding to one another. This involves bringing people together under circumstances reasonably free of noise, clarifying the rules governing the decoding processes, and assuring that people will listen to and hear what has been said before they respond. A major responsibility is that of teaching the participants to arrange for feedback and pay attention to its implications.

THE DECISION-MAKING FUNCTION

Decision-making is a central responsibility of leaders who must make choices themselves and introduce processes by which members can decide issues. There is no substitute for courage in confronting issues, for risk is always present in some degree. A willingness to venture must be balanced by command of a rational process if group goals and individual needs of members are to be met.

Some fairly complex processes have been developed

and may be useful in varied endeavors. Most consist of attempts to describe how an intelligent person naturally approaches a choice. The suggestion offered here is simplicity itself and involves five steps easily remembered and quickly accomplished in most situations— though its subtleties may be elaborated in certain circumstances. The steps are: see, search, sort, shape, and settle.

See

The first step is to clarify the problem. What is it? Is the presenting issue the real problem or does it represent something else? Are there actually several problems wrapped up together which ought to be separated for effective treatment? What are the most probable causes of the problem? Do they suggest what really needs to be decided? How important is the issue? Is it central or peripheral? Does it have to be settled if the organization is to continue, and meet its goals and the needs of its members? Is it, rather, an opportunity for a desirable development? When the problem is clearly defined and given priority, one is ready for the next step.

Search

Search behavior is directed to developing possibilities. The quality of a decision is likely to be enhanced as the number of possible alternatives is increased. When one chooses among ten solutions, there is a greater chance that the winner will be appropriate than when the decision is between two. In a few situations this is a luxury beyond our means, but thoughtful searching often produces a remarkable assortment of choices. One major value of computers is their capacity to store an immense bank of different ideas which may be recalled instantly to supply alternatives in the face of a given situation. It is important to remember that computers are mechanical copies of the human brain, which is superbly equipped for information storage and retrieval. Experienced leaders have a large deposit of useful data in their memory banks. Since much of the required material is in the subconscious area, successful decision makers often seem to act intuitively. Others have learned that for major decisions it is wise to give the subconscious a chance, so they postpone action until there has been time for the process to work. This is also a valid reason for deciding weighty matters at a second meeting rather than at the one where the issues are initially presented. It is useful in such a circumstance to articulate this reason for delay and in this—as in every situation calling for decision—to encourage the habit of searching for possibilities.

Sort

The next step is sorting the possibilities, including the possibility of doing nothing. Each is given a priority level in terms of the extent to which it solves the problem, with a look at probable results and side effects (desirable or unfortunate), the cost in time and money and the availability of personnel and other resources.

Shape

The most promising possibilities are then shaped by borrowing from others, adding or removing features, and adjusting cost and personnel factors. Features may be changed to reduce the risks of unfavorable side effects or plans developed for contingent actions which could mitigate unfortunate impacts on persons.

Settle

The final step is decisive action. If all that has gone before has been well done, a person or a group should approach this act with some confidence. However, it has been assumed in this description of a process that the individual or the group is acting rationally, has access to adequate information, and is performing in an environment that is receptive. We know that there will always be some irrational factors. To the extent that they influence the process, there will be less chance of decisions which support the organization goals. The major resource for dealing with this problem is the character-building power of the Christian faith and the pastoral care available to members.

To meet the unpredictability caused by incomplete information and unfriendly or turbulent environment, game theorists have suggested the principle of "mini-max." They observe that the best gain over the longest period of time is probably to be achieved by decisions not directed at maximum gain, nor settling for minimums, but aimed somewhat in between. This is obviously true in financial matters, but it is surprisingly relevant in developing a program or in dealing with persons or groups.[21]

DEALING WITH CHANGE

Most decisions involve change for someone, and people resist being changed. They have their own ideas about what should be done, and often use potent strategies against individuals or groups that try to change them.

A great deal has been written about the minister or church officer as change agent. Every group needs information about the techniques available and the almost infinite variety of possibilities open to them, together with data on effects experienced by others. They also need skilled help in developing chosen approaches, learning to use the processes required, and securing wide participation. Perhaps most of all, they need at the start—and often in subsequent beginnings—encouragement and support in approaching change in ways that seem costly, if the hidden costs of rough-and-ready ways are unnoticed.

Change is a continuing fact of life. The Greek philosopher Heraclitus long ago observed that "everything flows."[22] This means, among other things, that the most determined efforts to keep every living thing as it is will be doomed to failure from the outset. Even if one living entity could perform the miracle of remaining the same, its meaning and behavior would be changed by the different relationships forced upon it by changes in other things.

Our choice is whether to plan change in the light of our convictions or to let it happen to us. Planned

change should result in activities rationally directed toward chosen goals. It will, however, have side effects
which are usually difficult and occasionally impossible
to forecast. The difficulty should not keep us from trying
to calculate the risks and make contingency plans.
Change that just happens to us or is initiated by an
impulsive individual will also have side effects, which
may be unfortunate; but there will be no chance to
prepare coping devices, and even the major thrust of
the new arrangement will have no rational relation to
our goals. While by happy chance there may be a desirable result, it is just as likely to be unwanted.

Part of the resistance to change is based on the intui-
tion that a certain degree of stability is essential for
healthy individual and social living. Scientific evidence
is piling up to the effect that too many changes coming
too close together often result in grave illness. In one
study, a psychiatrist devised a scale on the basis of wide
testing which assigned point values to thirty-nine
changes. They ranged from the death of a spouse (100
points) or a divorce (73 points) through a marriage (50
points) or a mortgage foreclosure (30 points) to a change
in residence (20 points). When an individual ran up
three hundred points within a year, there was an 80
percent chance of pathological depression, heart attack,
or other serious ailment. Of scorers in the 150–300
range, 53 percent were similarly affected, as were 33
percent of those scoring up to 150. This unhappy picture set against the backdrop of the kaleidoscopic turn-
over of everything in our time depicted by Toffler in
Future Shock suggests that the cost of change may
sometimes be more than most of us can afford.[23]

The evidence is strong that the church often serves

well as a support structure for people in the midst of barely tolerable strains. That structure, too, will change. The people within it should be able to stand more change than those outside, but they also have limited tolerance for stress. Leaders must keep this in mind and count the cost as they fulfill their responsibilities for initiating change.

How to Change Things

It may be useful to explore ways of effecting change, since leaders must deal with conditions that prevent groups from fulfilling their purposes or fail to sustain individual development.

One obvious way to change things is to *suppress the opposition.* This may be done openly by a person who has the necessary physical or political power. It may also be done by manipulative techniques designed to bypass the minds of those otherwise disposed to resist. A monopoly of the sources of information can be arranged, so that there is no access to contradictory opinions or reports of unfortunate results. There can be subtle use of social rewards and punishments, or the engineering of small-group pressures.

Church leaders can see the iniquity of such techniques when they are used by communists for "brainwashing." They may not be as revolted by similar practices in some kinds of revival meetings or organized demonstrations, or high-pressure small-group activities under ecclesiastical auspices. The Christian imperative is respect for whole persons and their right freely to make choices. God's entire family purpose for the universe is in a small degree subverted when one attempts to effect change by suppressing the opposition. The heavenly Father would not even use this technique to save his Son from the cross!

Our occasional efforts to follow this route are tragic. If successful, they diabolically twist out of shape the Christian intention they were designed to serve. We soon learn, moreover, that the universe and the people in it are so made that suppression rarely has a long-term effectiveness.

Sometimes *negotiation* is a sound way to deal with those who resist change. If the parties involved represent roughly equal strength, bargaining may be possible —and when there is unequal power, persuasion can be important. Agreement will depend in no small degree upon the skill of the one who moderates the discussions in drawing out the positions of the contestants. If a church leader is advocating a change, he or she will be well advised to arrange for someone else to referee the exchanges.

Negotiation is at home in the Christian context, since it assumes mutual respect and an openness to the truth.

Limited conflict develops when even Christians of goodwill are unable to compose their differences about the wisdom of change or its appropriateness. Since there is no halfway station between change and no change, the most amiable persons sometimes find themselves in conflict. The intelligent question is not how to make the difference go away, but how to carry on the conflict within such limits that persons and groups are not harmed—while a constructive course of action is determined. The solution that the human race has developed is a highly programmed, ritualistic sort of conflict. We see this in debate, in arbitration efforts, in the courtroom, and in parliamentary procedure. The synagogues of our Lord's day in Palestine were accustomed to this approach. We find the Jerusalem Council gathering to deal with changes proposed by the apostle Paul (Acts 15:6–29)—and changes have been decided upon by church councils up through Vatican II and recent World Council of Churches meetings.

In local churches, ideas for change are often discussed in parliamentary fashion within official boards, committees, and organizations, as well as in congregational meetings. Where people are accustomed to such procedures, it is possible to have strong differences of opinion and still come to decisions by majority rule without harm to anyone—and with advantage to the cause. However, when tension over change continues through several meetings, some unfortunate things are likely to occur. The groups involved tend to close their minds to information that does not support their position, and to exalt the officers who agree with them and vilify opposition leaders. If they win, they are likely to be trapped in the winning structures and cling to them when they are no longer appropriate. If they lose, they may devote too much energy to winning the next time or turn to scapegoating someone.

It is not surprising that churches have become interested in *planning and problem-solving* approaches to change. These processes open the way for all concerned to bring to bear on any proposal for change all the resources of mind and heart and experience in the light of the Christian gospel and the mission of the church. While consensus may prove beyond reach and a parliamentary decision may be essential, those who participate will come to the moment of choice better prepared. In this approach, all the persons to be affected by a decision are introduced to the steps in the process at the outset so that they may take creative parts.

The first step is developing mutuality and trust. Sometimes this is a "given." The group is well acquainted. They have studied the Bible together and prayed for each other and worked side by side. Sometimes the relationships have never gone below the surface, and it will not be wasteful to spend time in talking about the experiences most satisfying or important to each member. When a major change is under consideration, many of the existing groups in the congregation may have a level of trust among their members which will make them suitable places for consideration of the possibilities if a plan can be developed to bring their insights together. Church leaders who care about people and trust them to be creative will be catalysts in this crucial first step.

The second step is unfreezing present attitudes. People who trust each other can begin to ask whether their commitment to the status quo would be modified or abandoned if an alternative offered satisfactions not now available. They can look at fears about a change and decide whether they should be determinative or whether they may be offset by advantages. They may visit places where the change is in effect, read about the experiences of others, or invite persons willing to evaluate their own experience of the change under consideration. They may discuss the possibilities among themselves and with other persons in the church. If, after a time, they find a lessening commitment to things as they are and an interest in developing something better, it may be said that the situation is "unfrozen" and the next step may be taken.

Planning is probably the best way to approach change. It begins by asking the theological question: What are we trying to do? It offers a process in which all can participate. It provides logical steps leading from a clarification of purpose to action. Because it begins with the gospel instead of with alternate programs, it is nonthreatening and open-ended. It makes the unfreezing process painless because needs for change appear evident wherever Christian purposes and present conditions are brought together and do not meet. The details of the process are spelled out in the next chapter.

COPING WITH CONFLICT

Conflict is evil if it hurts persons without opening possibilities for their redemption or renders it impossible for the church, which is the body of Christ, to carry forward its mission. While the Bible assures us that God can make the wrath of man to praise him, the family concept of the universe which dominates the Christian revelation places great stress on the blessedness of peacemaking. It is an essential responsibility of the Christian leader to join the Lord in prayer that all may be one (John 17:21) and to do what can be done toward this purpose. Paul, writing to the Corinthians, was not the last Christian leader to mourn over the harm done to individuals and to the body of Christ by divisions and quarrels (I Cor. 1:10–17ff.). Like the apostle, the pastor and the church officer need to cultivate the peacemaker's art and know how to remind the faithful that their Master prayed for those who despitefully used him.

It is important, however, to notice that it is not differences of viewpoint that hurt and destroy, but the failure of love which results in vicious hostility. Jesus tells us to love our enemies (Matt. 5:14; Luke 6:27, 35), but he nowhere insists that we share their views. He himself more than once entered upon conflict because he believed it essential to uphold the truth. What he would *not* do was to attempt the destruction of those who disagreed with him.

Disagreement that results in open confrontation can be creative and fully congruent with Christian commitment. Such conflict may force both parties to reexamine opinions and procedures. It may also develop pressure which stirs vigorous motivation for learning.

When a Christian community expects some divergences of view and occasional confrontations among its members, pressures to conform are reduced and members feel free to explore novel ideas, procedures, and techniques. Conflict may thus become the scaffolding for a more creative church.

7

Leaders Involve
People in Planning

Planning is an essential first step in ministry. The processes involved may be used in laying out projects as different as a sermon or a campaign, a service of worship or a building, a single prayer meeting or a twelve-year educational curriculum. In this chapter we have elected to watch the development of a long-range planning process in a local church. The assumption is that once the steps are clear, anyone can use them in simplified form for enterprises of more modest scope.

FAITH AND PLANNING

Jesus began his ministry with thirty days in the wilderness. During that time he clarified his purpose, examined the prospect before him, faced problems, explored possibilities, decided on a program, and established a pattern of action. Over and over in the brief ministry that followed, he drew aside to pray and to plan.

It is no accident that planning has a place of importance in Western culture which, as much as it has distorted the Christian world view, still inherits some of

Christianity's salient characteristics. One of them is a basic conviction that human beings can have a real part in shaping the future. This view cannot survive in a fatalistic atmosphere. Hope is an essential element of an environment that is to be favorable to planning. At long last the world is a rough place for hope without faith in the risen Christ and the assurance he brings about the character of God and the future which is in his hands. "The prospect of this future," Jürgen Moltmann has written, "opens up here and now an open space of change and freedom which must be shaped with responsibility and confidence."[24] This Christian hope becomes an active, if somewhat critical, partner of planning. Jesus is critical of the fussy concern about the future which, in the fear born of faithlessness, fills today with nightmares about tomorrow. He is even less enthusiastic about those who begin enterprises or buildings without counting the cost and suggests harsh judgment for those, like the lamp-carrying bridesmaids without reserves, who do not plan ahead. (Matt. 25: 1–13; Luke 14:28–32.)

Planning is no substitute for prayer, or for the guidance of the Spirit of God. Prayer is a pervasive aspect of the Christian life, for we live in constant dependence on God and with an underlying assurance that we are in his presence. The New Testament gives us confidence that we can embark on enterprises in which he is interested, may speak to him about them, and expect his guidance and support. Prayer, then, has a place of importance in all that we do, including efforts at planning. His Spirit is our guide at all times, but he does not offer this guidance as a substitute for thought or for hard work. There are occasions when he acts powerfully in ways entirely surprising to us, but most of the time he works through the powers with which he has endowed us. As a matter of fact, he never bypasses our minds the way some advertisers try to do—because they do not respect us as persons—and he does respect us. We should have seen this at the cross, which would have been entirely unnecessary had he been willing to treat us as things and supply our thoughts for us. This he will not do. He expects us to think and plan to the best of our ability. It is no less trusting to seek his guidance months ahead of an event than at the instant it happens, if the earlier application enables us better to use the powers he has given us. We need also to remember that our small minds and sinful inclinations limit what he can do through us. However willing his help, we are left with imperfect apprehensions of the prospect before us and with plans that, however useful, are in some respects out of date by the time they are made. We can never make blueprints of the future. Planning is always in the context of hope—not sight—but it is a great deal better than no planning at all, and it has a sure place in the life of faith.

Planning has another strong alliance with the Christian viewpoint, for it is a friend of change. Our Lord has taught us to pray, "Thy kingdom come . . . on earth" (Matt. 6:10), and no one of us is so blind as to suppose this can happen without major changes. When we become his disciples changes begin to take place in us, and this process continues as long as we live. The theologians describe the process as "sanctification," which means, literally, "making holy" or shaping us more and more into his image. This process is as much needed in our life together as in our individual lives; there must be never-ending changes in our corporate life, which is to say in our institutions. Too often the church exempts itself from this process and tends to become a quaint relic with limited relevance. Some members enjoy this and wish to preserve things as they are, because the church becomes for them a refuge from the world—a quiet pool off to the side where they can escape the turbulence of swift-flowing days. Other members are impatient with the church and are inclined to tell the congregation how wrong it is, or to force change by vigorous action which is disowned by the majority. These strategies, however satisfying to the individuals, are painfully ineffectual. The preservers of the status quo do not find in the caricature they have made of the church the stimulus to growth they need, nor the ministry the world needs. If they do not wake up to this, their children usually do. On the other hand, the impatient soon discover—if they have any sensitivity—that "telling people" is a somewhat futile effort when the targets are not motivated to listen. Forcing people to be parties to action only creates resistance. Most of us will fight being changed by someone else, though we may be less reluctant to take part in change. The planning process is a means by which we can all discover together whether change is called for by our Lord, and can all have a part in developments that may be required.

Planning is also the best defense against goal displacement, which can so easily develop in any organization. The church, in common with organizations of all sorts, has both a corporate mission and a capacity to meet the individual needs of members. Individual needs are so pressing that they tend to take precedence over the goals of the united enterprise to the extent that the group mission becomes less and less important. Further, individuals are inclined to identify with the institution instead of its mission, so that its maintenance and perpetuation assumes primary importance. The drives involved in this subversion are much too strong to be overcome by protest and will easily circumvent most external strategies. It is only as members are involved in a process in which the common purpose is clarified and given a central place that they perceive the extent to which their self-centered concerns have twisted the church out of shape, and may be prepared to do something about it.

Planning has strategic value for the church, though it is a resource capable of application in many other areas by both individuals and groups. It may be used by one person to structure a week, or to lay out a sermon or a series, or to develop a study program. It may be employed by an organization to set up a sales campaign or to staff an office, or prepare for a picnic or a crisis. It may be undertaken by a whole church or one of its organizations. It may apply to a single enterprise, such as the development of a new venture in worship, a different educational activity, a staff change, an evangelistic or social action project; or it may be used to plan a whole year's activities or those of a decade.

We will discuss the process in terms of plans for a church year, assured that readers can simplify for smaller undertakings or enlarge for more ambitious efforts. The church year offers a canvas large enough that details become clear, and the main outlines stand out and become familiar. Further, only an enterprise of this size is likely to give rise to serious concentration on the basic purpose and prospect of the particular church, which is essential background for the more modest planning efforts.

PARTICIPATORY PLANNING: WHY AND HOW

Our congregation has come together in response to the love of God in Christ and we intend, in accordance with his commission, to minister to each other and to the world. Among us there is a wide diversity of gifts, and in order to use them all effectively it is necessary to have leadership that will provide for continual communication, and for the decisions that must be made. One way to provide for this is to put all the responsibility and power in the hands of one person. This leader then sees to it that everyone knows what to do.

Suppose, however, we believe that God's Spirit tends to speak more clearly through groups, since in them individual self-interests are balanced, blind spots are overcome, and creativity is stimulated by cross-fertilization. Suppose we know, further, that people are highly motivated to do things when they have taken part in choosing goals and activities. It then becomes important to develop a kind of leadership that can be shared. The individual leader has his or her function, but rather than telling people what to do, the task is to introduce the group to processes that make corporate leadership possible.

One of these processes is planning. It lends itself to extensive participation. Where a large number of persons is involved, as in a congregation, it should be immediately apparent that individuals or small groups will have to work between the larger meetings. In fact, a rhythm should emerge: the step is discussed, then the individual or small group does the required research and shapes the possible alternatives for decision by the larger assembly; then the next step is discussed, and so forth. In many denominations local churches elect governing boards that are responsible for leadership, and hence perform the planning function. This is acceptable to members of the congregation, and for ordinary routines it works very well. But when it comes to plans for a major program, a costly project, or a real change, participation on a much wider scale can mean the difference between failure and success. We are not talking about an opportunity to "rubberstamp" a set of proposals all worked out, but rather a real involvement at each step of the process.

Pastors and officers occasionally speak of the unwillingness of large numbers of Christians to participate in ministry. Clearly, the problem is motivation. People are generally indifferent—though polite—about plans made by others. The right question, then, is how to involve members in the planning process.

One possibility is to begin with a small planning committee or task force in the official board. They survey the steps of the process and develop a preliminary time sequence, figuring into it all the meetings and actions that will be required. Then they lead the official board through the experience they have had and propose that, without committing itself further, the board begin with the first step, the clarification of purpose. When the board has agreed on a tentative statement of purpose for the congregation, board members visit each of the other organizations in the church to ask for criticism and assistance in arriving at an adequate declaration. The board may also—or instead—call meetings of members after church services or mail the statements with requests for response. One board trained visitors to take the statements into homes for discussions. When a broad consensus has been reached and the board adopts a tentative statement of purpose, the second step in the planning process is carried forward in the same way, and so on through the sequence.

Another approach is to have a small committee explore the planning process and then explain it to the chairpersons of the working committees of the board. These leaders are asked to explore the process with the members of their committees, who presumably consist of a fairly wide cross section of the congregation. Each board committee is then asked to develop a proposed plan for its area, including in the planning stages persons they hope may have a part in implementing the plan. On a target date, announced well in advance, all the participants in the planning meet with the board for a day-long session in which proposals are made and the board adopts an overall plan.

A third possibility is extensive work in the governing board on the purpose of the congregation, followed by a sermon on the subject and an invitation to each member to join a task force that will explore each of the steps in planning, with periodic meetings of the groups for communication and joint recommendations, and a final convocation to put it all together.

STEPS IN THE PLANNING PROCESS

The steps in the planning process are the clarification of *purpose,* the analysis of the *prospect,* the identification of *problems* or concerns, the listing of *possibilities,* the choice of *projects* or programs, and, finally, the development of a *pattern* of action. These stages in a process have as their background John Dewey's analysis of how we think,[25] a heritage they share with virtually all descriptions of decision-making. They are commended as easily grasped, readily applied, and sufficiently memorable to be used for frequent reference. The process they describe looks like this outline:

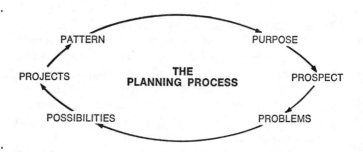

Let us now explore each step.

Step 1. The Clarification of Purpose

This is a theological task which each church must perform for itself, relying, of course, on the Bible and on the confessions developed by thoughtful Christians through the ages. It will also be worthwhile to notice what the church has actually done in each period of its history and on each continent under the leading of the Holy Spirit. This should suggest avenues for legitimate ministry and avoid blind alleys in which activity can only bring frustration, or worse.

The clarification of purpose is of crucial importance because the emergent statement will have within it the seeds of all that is to be done and will form the referent for choosing projects, establishing priorities, and evaluating results. Vague generalizations or the dodging of issues at this point will cripple the entire enterprise. Furthermore, this effort can have value beyond its immediate utility in encouraging members to think theologically, developing a Christian perspective on the church and the world which may affect all their behavior.

It is assumed that this first step will be a group enterprise, not a clerical exercise. There is no other point in the planning process at which the minister as the theologian-in-residence is better equipped to assist. The task of the pastoral theologian is not to do our thinking for us but to introduce us to sources and ways of approaching issues. In some churches this process can be completed in two or three months of hard work; in others, the decision is made to continue with "business as usual" for six or twelve months while the purpose is clarified, first by the official board, and then by a good percentage of the membership.

The Bible does not provide prepackaged purpose statements. It is a record of the inspired reflections of men and women who experienced the presence of God and came to know his grace. They sought to record their experiences and to respond to the grace. They did not speak with one voice, but each, guided by the Spirit, has a unique and important contribution to make. Together, they give a variety of suggestions that can help spark a discovery of purpose for your congregation in its particular situation.

Here are some passages that may be useful: Genesis 12:1–3 and Hebrews 11:8–16; Exodus 3:13–17 and Matthew 28:18–20; Deuteronomy 6:4–9; Isaiah 11:-1–9; Isaiah 53; Isaiah 61:1–4 and Luke 4:18–19; Jeremiah 7:1–15; Matthew 25:31–46; Mark 8:27–38; John 3:16–20; John 8:31–36; John 10:7–18; Romans 12:1–21; I Corinthians 12:4–31; II Corinthians 4 and 5:16–21; Ephesians 2:11–22 and 4:1–16; Colossians 3:12–17; I John 2:7–11.

It may also be worthwhile to look at history, since the Holy Spirit has guided the church through the centuries. We may ask questions like these: What has the church always done when it was healthy? What are the most vital churches doing today?

Some of the value words in the last paragraph can be cleared up only by theological answers. When is a church "healthy" or "vital"? For answers to questions of this sort, we turn to the theological consensus of God's people found in the great confessions. Whatever our denomination, we have access to carefully reasoned statements based on Scripture and tested in the life of the communion.

Even a cursory review of ecclesiastical history will make it plain that the church has always been engaged in at least three kinds of activity: worship, mutual nurture, and witness or mission. In different periods and places one or another of these has occupied a larger place, but each has been involved. There are those who in their desire to emphasize a theological point would insist that one of these three activities is the mission of the church and the others contributory, which may or may not be the case. The important fact is that the people of God, calling upon his Spirit for guidance, have always been led to do these things. Whatever our method of developing a statement of purpose for our church, we will probably not go far wrong if it includes variations on these themes.

One congregation, after extended effort, with wide participation, evolved the following tentative statement which was approved by the official board and used as a basis for the other steps in planning:

I. Worship—God has made man in his image, and wants a personal relationship with us. In worship, we express what we think and feel about God, confident that he wants such communication to exist. We listen to God, using the sermon, Scriptures, Sacraments, and service of worship to discover his will. We present to God the needs of men and the world, in the belief that God will bring love and justice to the world. Worship culminates in the recommitting of ourselves to God for growth and service.

II. Nurture—God wants us to live together as his family. In his church, he wants us to care for each other, teach each other, and work with each other. Nurture means encouraging friendships and mutual support, developing values and conveying information about the Christian faith and life, and involving people in meaningful church activities.

III. Mission—God has brought a worldwide church into existence and wants us to serve him by ministering to the needs of men. Our Lord, Jesus Christ, has charged us to go into the world to preach, teach, heal, and help those who are struggling with destructive forces. Thus, the church serves God and the world by making his love and power known through a variety of missions which reconcile men to God and to each other.

This declaration is not included as an ideal statement of purpose, but as a position paper which represented a certain stage of development in the theological views of a group and a series of compromises, particularly in the third section. It is not as specific as some would like to make it, but it has stood up rather well in use as a program guide and norm for evaluation. It has also been useful as program groups have sought to clarify subsidiary purposes and develop specific goals.

Step 2. Analysis of the Prospect

The prospect includes the situation and assumptions about the future in regard to both the congregation and its community, seen in the light of the established purposes. The activities required are research and analysis. These things are usually done by individuals or small task forces, then reported to the larger group for consensus.

Data About the Church

The research includes data-gathering about the church in such areas as

a. Membership: each member's age, sex, marital status, education, occupation, income, interests.
b. Programs: estimates of the percentage of the congregation involved weekly, monthly, or occasionally. The relationship of the activities to the church's pur-

pose. Their effectiveness in terms of their goals, and reasonable projections of the future of each program for one, five, and ten years. The list should include (1) services of worship; (2) educational programs; (3) personal growth and fellowship programs; (4) pastoral care programs, including counseling and visits by members and staff; (5) evangelistic programs with records of persons touched and percentage of response; (6) social action programs with listing of projects, relationships, and effects; (7) ecumenical programs, with indication of sharing in local, regional, national and worldwide interrelated work of the church; (8) personnel programs for recruiting and training leaders; (9) support programs dealing with (i) buildings (space, furniture, and equipment available for present and future programs, their adequacy, adaptability, condition, and the number of hours' use in an average week of seventy hours, with policies for maintenance, replacement, and new acquisitions); (ii) finances (adequacy for programs, comparison of budget with churches of similar size and composition, per capita giving compared to other congregations, per family giving compared to average family income in the church's area); (iii) stewardship (methods used compared with and evaluated against methods used by other congregations); (iv) public relations (use of bulletins, newsletters, outdoor signs, releases to newspapers, radio, advertisements).

Information About the Community
Information about the community around the church may include:

1. Character: rural, town, suburban, urban; primary use

for residence, farming, commerce, industry.
2. Extent: number of members within ½ mile, 1 mile, 3 miles, etc.; area for which church takes responsibility and in what ways.
3. Population: growing, static, declining; number of families and persons; census tracts involved; age, sex, marital status, racial and ethnic backgrounds, education, occupation, income, religious preferences and church affiliations.
4. Housing: type (single-family, duplex, apartments); average age, condition; cost or rental; availability of land for building and effect of zoning restrictions; percentage of annual mobility and source of newcomers.
5. Dominant influences, major problems, and ways in which the community, as described in this survey, is likely to change in one, five, and ten years.
6. Churches of the same or a different denomination, their particular character and constituencies, cooperative endeavors, and ecumenical interests.

Putting It Together

Analysis of the prospect includes an effort to bring together the emerging pictures of the church and its area. In what ways are the people in the congregation like those in the community? In what ways do they differ? And what does this mean? Given the resources available now or in the future, is the church addressing itself to an area of appropriate size, with needed programs which have some chance of success? What trends or expected changes in the community will affect the church?

This effort at synthesis, which may include some comparative charts, will lead naturally into the next step.

Step 3. Identifying the Problems

Problems or concerns emerge when purposes and prospects are brought together. The purposes serve as measures against which existing conditions and probable developments may be weighed, tested, and evaluated. At the points where the purposes and prospects do not coincide, problems or concerns appear.

Worship Problem

If, for example, we declare that "God . . . wants a personal relationship with us" which is expressed in worship, and we discover that a substantial number of members or neighbors do not worship regularly, there is a problem that needs to be identified. Limited attendance may indicate that a certain percentage of the congregation is infirm and cannot leave home for any reason, or that a number are required to work on Sundays, or that quite a few must travel on business, or that a substantial group are away on weekends for recreation. It may be that some find limited appeal in a particular form of worship (or certain elements in it), or in the hours in which services are available. Others may be kept from worship by personal or marital difficulties or financial problems. Others may face so many difficulties in belief that they would rather avoid the subject of religion.

Nurture Problem

If we assert that "God wants us to live together as his family," and we learn that a number of our members and larger numbers of neighbors live for months on end without meaningful fellowship, there is an obvious problem or concern. The church may have inadequate provisions for fellowship, such as small personal groups for individuals or couples, prayer and Bible study circles, social hours after services, work projects, and special events. Possibly the quality of Christian experience developed is so limited in its vertical dimension that it scarcely has horizontal thrust. Active persons may be so preoccupied as to be blind to the isolation of those ignored; or so insecure in their own importance that they unconsciously reject others who may possibly displace them. Perhaps old friends are so glad to see each other that they have no eyes for newcomers. Or newcomers and old-timers, alike, are shy and feel awkward about meeting others. The congregation may be so inclusive that miracles are needed to bridge the gaps between persons of very different capacities, experiences, and interests.

Mission Problem

If we state that "Our Lord, Jesus Christ, has charged us to go into the world to preach, teach, heal, and help those who are struggling with destructive forces" and at the same time observe that most of our members are not individually or corporately engaged in evangelism or social action, we cannot avoid the conclusion that the church has a problem, or should have a concern. It may be that a number of members feel they do not know enough to share their faith, or they may be so uncertain about their beliefs that they avoid discussing them. Possibly social pressures intimidate them, or the fear of being thought hypocrites deters them. There may be no structures by which they can prepare themselves to join others in speaking of their convictions. It is likely that some are not clear about the relationship between Christian faith and social action, or make no connection between community service and their religious commitment. Again, the church may provide too few channels for social action.

Other Problems or Concerns

We have listed a few problems to suggest a style of approach. Others will emerge as the membership is compared with the surrounding population and trends are identified. Gaps appear as programs are set over against purposes, compared to those in other churches, and weighed against needs. Concerns may develop as the quality and morale and adequacy of leaders is examined, and the availability and use of resources is considered.

Some churches have published the tentative statement of purpose and a summary of the prospect approved by the official board, asking members to suggest any revisions but particularly to identify the problems or concerns that seem important to them. This request has been mailed to members with a reply envelope. Some committees have felt that the mail approach may create a morale problem by emphasizing problems, and if used should be preceded by a Sunday presentation. Others have invited members to special gatherings after services, or have made presentations at each of the organizations during a month, or combined several of these arrangements. Often, to accentuate the positive, the planning committee has, at the same time, asked for contributions to the fourth step: listing the possibilities. Either before going to the whole membership or immediately afterward, the committee has arranged through the official board for a meeting of that board with all other board members and leaders of particular organizations for a day or half a day to consider a summary of the first, second, and third steps (which has been mailed out in advance), and secure the crucial suggestions required in the fourth step.

Step 4. Listing the Possibilities

Once a problem or concern is identified, the next step is the listing of possibilities. The gap between the straight line of the purpose and the jagged edge of the prospect may have many solutions. It is of the utmost importance that a number of possibilities be discovered. A group that chooses two projects from twenty-five possibilities will almost certainly have better projects than if the choice is limited to two out of four—or worse, out of two.

A small planning committee will wish to develop as many ideas as it can, then enlist an ever-widening circle in the effort. We have already suggested a sequence beginning with the official board, moving through a day together for all officers and leaders, and including in some way as many members as possible. Those gathered may hear an overall report from the committee, then break up into small groups to consider general possibilities. This may be followed by committee presentations covering particular areas such as worship, nurture–pastoral care, nurture–education, witness–evangelism, witness–social action, and supporting activities. After the suggestions have been discussed briefly, there may be small groups dealing with all the areas, or an opportunity to meet with a small group working on one of the areas. A second chance to send in other suggestions is likely to be fruitful, since creative ideas frequently emerge after people brood over or "sleep on" problems, giving the subconscious opportunity to process materials and come up with imaginative and, possibly, innovative proposals.

Possibilities may emerge through the discovery of what others have done in similar circumstances. Books, articles in periodicals, suggestions from denominational or ecumenical agencies, visits, or mail inquiries may prove fruitful. One committee listed all the proposals that came to their attention, then sought information about successful use of each of these ideas. They invited individuals who appeared to be responsible for the successes to come and share their enthusiasm and expertise. Members of the congregation were urged to hear the visitors, who were called "advocates," and to indicate how much interest they felt in the projects described.

The crucial point in all of this is that good planning always includes the production of many more possibilities than the group can use, so that real choices are available.

Here are some suggestions:

Worship Possibilities

Worship possibilities may come to light if we take a new look at the places in which we gather. Should the sanctuary be rearranged? Does the location of the chancel furniture fit our theology and psychology? Would it help or hinder if we used brighter colors on the walls, growing plants and trees, informal music, different instruments, banners, hangings, posters, projected film? Would we feel more like a family gathered together if the seating brought us face-to-face, or would a change of this sort be simply disturbing?

Should some of our services be in completely different settings: other rooms in the building or in homes, so that we can experiment with seating, encourage informal dress, and adjust more easily to new sights and sounds?

Is it possible that our participation in the Sacraments can be enriched by different arrangements or variations in style, or by offering such things for some, while others enjoy rituals hallowed by years of repetition?

What about times of worship? If a significant proportion of our membership must work on Sunday mornings, or if many persons are away at summer or winter play or are traveling on business, should there be opportunities for worship during the week? When? Or will a move of this sort further weaken the idea of the Sabbath which has made a place for religion in a busy world?

Then there are questions of form and content. Would all our services benefit from changes in materials and style, greater use of ancient prayers and liturgies, new forms, prayers with different pronouns, more frequent use of recently composed hymns and contemporary anthems? What about sermons that include dialogue or are in other ways open-ended? Is there a place for rituals that involve more contact of eye and hand, more movement and free expression—or would things like these make us conscious of forms instead of conscious of God?

What about family services in informal settings for those who prefer them, with father and mother and children, including the smallest, taking turns in leadership? Some churches have groups of twenty to a hundred who meet this way every Sunday, and have very rich experiences. Often, they include individuals or fragments of families who, in this way, come to feel very much a part of family life in the church.

Are we doing all we can for shut-ins: offers of transportation to services, tape recordings, broadcasts of services?

How do visitors feel among us? Are there ways, without artificial heartiness or sentimentality, to let them know they are welcome? Is the fellowship after services genuine and inclusive? Are there things that could be done to make it more so?

Nurture Possibilities

Nurture possibilities may appear if we examine our arrangements for pastoral care, and Christian education, and fellowship.

How can we make more adequate provisions for pastoral care? Should we be training church officers or volunteers for this task? The elders or deacons in many churches are serving as pastors to the people, calling in the minister only when the situation requires expertise they have not yet acquired. The plan requires constant on-the-job training which takes up so much time at monthly meetings that boards or committees without policy-making responsibilities can usually manage it better than official board members. Other individuals or task forces may be especially equipped by experience and have special training to care for shut-ins, deal with marital problems, or sit with troubled relatives while loved ones are in operating rooms. Some may be prepared to give vocational guidance and help in finding jobs, or support the bereaved.

What are the possibilities before us in Christian education? Are there ways we could encourage much larger numbers of the adult members to study their faith and its implications? Should there be classes on Sunday or during the week? Should we offer some of the new programmed instruction materials to interested persons? Is there a way to promote the reading of religious books from the church library or the public library through attractive annotated bibliographies on various subjects, references in services, noticeable displays, or special classes? Can we get people to recognize in newspapers and novels and movies and television shows the great themes of the faith: God's love; sin and salvation; despair and hope? Would the institution of some small groups help with this, or new emphases in church school teaching, or brief discussions at board and organization meetings? If adults find it hard to enroll in study or personal groups meeting over a full year, should we have short-term courses or offer weekend or one-day retreats at the church—or away, somewhere?

What about activities that bring together religion and art, such as art festivals or courses; or projects dealing with poetry, music, graphics, painting, sculpture, photography, and dance?

Possibilities for children and youth are legion: schools and classes, retreats and camps and conferences, audiovisuals and celebrations, open classrooms with the older helping to teach the younger (and growing in the process). We can choose from a galaxy of curriculum materials, small-group approaches taking the place of recreation-centered activity, and social action projects of all kinds. Should we also ask whether the church can help to narrow the generation gap by including whole families in mutual education and fellowship groups instead of traditional grouping of age levels in church schools? What would happen if ten families met at church each week, with old and young working together to appropriate and live out the new life in Christ?

Have we such provisions for fellowship that most of our members are associated with at least a dozen other members who value and trust and warmly affirm and support one another? Are some of our groups too big? Should couples, for example, be in small groups of not more than fifteen pairs so they can meet in one another's homes? Should we have many small interpersonal fellowships meeting for regular Bible study, prayer, sharing of experiences, and social action? Are our men's and women's organizations serving real needs, or would it be better for men and women to be meeting together in small groups?

Mission Possibilities

Can we increase our impact in evangelism, the sharing of the good news about Christ? Do we need to train door-to-door canvassers, telephone callers, invitation callers, and persons who can sit down with a new friend and talk about faith?

In social action, should we have task forces concerned with services to families, youth, the aging, and minorities? Should we have, or encourage the community to have, programs for tutoring, for work with parolees, for improving courts and correctional procedures and facilities? Should something be done about self-determination among welfare recipients, and about better housing and living conditions? What provisions are being made for dealing with pollution, for urging ethical considerations in business and politics, for combating racism, for dealing with harmful drugs? Is anyone developing consultations on such issues as peace, international trade, taxes, voting rights, and participation in government? What are we doing for older people?

What should we be doing to advance the world mission of the church? Entertaining international students and fraternal workers? Establishing a mission center in the hall with a world map and literature? Conducting an annual mission conference or festival? Relating traveling members to Christian activities in the places they visit across America and around the world? Recruiting short-term workers and professionals to give a month or a summer? Adopting special support projects?

Supporting Activities Possibilities

If buildings are inadequate, should we increase the space available by having duplicate services or activities, or using community facilities? Should we have more worship, classes, or groups in homes, or develop a cluster arrangement with another church or churches? Would it be feasible to work out an arrangement for joint use of facilities with a community agency that needs only weekday space? Should we get along with present structures, add another, or replace everything? If there are areas of the building which are used only a few hours a week, could we minister to the city or the community, and possibly cut overhead, by inviting a number of agencies or groups to use space during the week on a cost basis? Possibilities might include a nursery school, an art center, offices for social agencies, a little theater, and meeting places for groups of all sorts. If the exterior is unattractive, should we reconstruct or replace it, or would imaginative landscaping call attention away from less fortunate appearances and give the important impression of vitality while leaving funds for all-important staff? If we are going to build, do community trends justify construction designed to last hundreds of years, or should we be exploring inexpensive possibilities? If finances are barely adequate, should we cut our programs—and if this is necessary, what do our purpose and prospect suggest about priorities? Would a planning/programming budget help in sorting priorities? Should we risk adding programs, and possibly staff, to meet a potentially dynamic prospect? Or should we develop a more effective stewardship effort? This might include year-round communication of information and cultivation of commitment. There could be major emphasis on giving a substantial proportion of income, possibly starting at 2 percent and moving toward 5 percent. Another feature often included is two-by-two calling on new members to explain proportionate giving and seek pledges. A good every-member canvass may involve a full quarter of the congregation in the calling and the training for it. Or would it be better to go on with the present stewardship plans and count on increased participation of members in meaningful Christian ministry to result in larger giving?

If a sampling indicates that neighbors do not know

the church exists, and visitors have trouble finding it, are there—beyond better programming—aspects of public relations that should have attention? (Signs at the church and at nearby intersections? News articles in the local paper and on radio programs? Advertisements designed to meet our prospect—to substitute for road signs in cities where these have limited value or are impossible; to call attention to events expected to have general interest; to appeal to persons for whom the church has a relevant message?)

Step 5. Picking Projects

When enough possibilities have been explored, the next step is the choice of projects or programs. We have already explored the decision-making process which involves seeing, searching, sorting, shaping, and settling. Usually, this effort makes for a clear priority list. On other occasions, a number of exciting opportunities cry out for action, and the official board, taking cognizance of all viewpoints and interests, votes to begin with some and keep the others for the future.

A useful device for weighing the claims of continuing programs and new possibilities is the process known as PPB (Planning—Programming—Budgeting), or sometimes as PBE (Planning—Budgeting—Evaluating).[26] There are four things to be done. First, we list the present line budget which has such items as salaries, oil, electricity, and insurance. Second, we list all programs of the church. Third, we figure what percentage of each line item is fairly chargeable to each program. For example, to the traditional morning worship, we charge 20 percent of the fuel item since it takes twenty dollars'

worth of fuel to heat the place of worship long enough
for the service, while the total fuel bill for the average
week is one hundred dollars. We also charge 30 percent
of the pastor's salary and fringe benefits, since he
devotes about one third of his time to preparation for
worship and preaching. Additional charges include 100
percent of the organist's remuneration, 20 percent of
the sexton's, 15 percent of the church secretary's, plus
100 percent of printing for the bulletin, and 60 percent
of the fire insurance since the place of worship represents 60 percent of the value covered. When this process is completed for each program, the entire amount
of the line budget has been allocated. The committee
is in a position to figure the cost of continuing any program and to calculate the effect of reducing, increasing,
or deleting it. We may also figure the redistribution,
increase, or decrease of expenditure involved in adding
or substituting a new program. Fourth, armed with this
information, we can decide whether a program's cost is
justified by the contribution it will make toward the
church's purpose.

PPB is a complex process and may appear more
objective than it is. Allocations are at best fairly
rough guesses and all the percentages are likely to
change whenever a program is added or deleted. It
is recommended particularly when the decision makers are rather sophisticated in finance and may be
tempted to shape the budget more on fiscal than
theological considerations.

Step 6. A Pattern of Action

Once the projects or programs have been chosen, the remaining step in planning is the development of a pattern of action. This is essential if anything is to happen. It includes:

A *structure* for carrying out the plan: a limited network of communication and decision, such as a committee, a commission, a task force, or an existing organization. A committee deliberates and brings proposals for action by the responsible body. A commission is delegated certain authority by the parent body so that it deliberates, acts, and reports its actions. A task force may be given committee or commission responsibilities but only for a clearly defined piece of work, and when that is accomplished, it goes out of existence. An existing organization may have quite different major responsibilities but be asked to serve in a particular matter with the authority of a committee or a commission.

A *personnel arrangement,* including job descriptions for participants, provisions for recruiting workers, and a training program. (These developments are all discussed in the next chapter.)

Provision for resources, including money and space and equipment. These may be allocated by the official board or may have to be secured in ways that should be spelled out. When money is involved, there should be a budget and accounting procedures. Space and equipment needs should be clearly specified in advance.

A *time frame* which estimates the time required for each activity in the pattern of action, and sets dates for the completion of each phase. This is often set up in chart form, with changes and adjustments made as necessary.[27] If this is done, the planners may avoid costly mistakes. It will be obvious, for example, that certain activities can proceed side by side, while others must follow a sequence in which one must be completed before another can begin.

Evaluation. This is comparatively easy if the first five steps in the planning process are faithfully carried out and a time frame is used. This part of the pattern of action sweeps across the top of our planning process wheel to look again at the purpose,

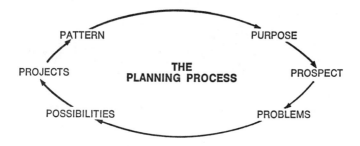

PATTERN   PURPOSE

PROJECTS   **THE PLANNING PROCESS**   PROSPECT

POSSIBILITIES   PROBLEMS

and review the entire process in the light of the results at the same time that the results are weighed in the light of the steps that led up to them. This may produce changes all along the line and should provide useful information when the process is undertaken for another year.

Celebration. When a plan has resulted in a worthwhile project or program, some recognition ought to be arranged on a scale commensurate with the accomplishment. This practice will contribute substantially to the development of morale in a congregation. Where it is followed regularly, the level of participation should rise. When planning results in change, celebration is an important part of general acceptance and the nurture of a sense of ownership of the new state of affairs.

SUMMARY

The planning process thus includes six steps: the clarification of purpose, the analysis of the prospect or situation, the identification of problems or concerns, the listing of possibilities, picking specific projects, and, finally, the development of a pattern of action.[28] When it is used in a congregation, the result should be an ever-larger percentage of the members acting as Christ's ministers, enthusiastically embarked on effective service to God and the world he loves.

8

Leaders Develop Other Leaders and Workers

The Holy Spirit endows the members of Christ's body with the gifts required for its healthy life and service in the world (I Cor. 1:7; 12:4–7, 11; Eph. 4:7; I Peter 4:10). Some are placed in the genes of members long before they are needed. Some arise in the interplay of native endowment with parental, societal, and environmental forces. And some emerge unexplained at turning points in a Christian's life. Frequently, talents lie buried until the church recognizes signs of their presence and corporately or through a leader calls the individual to answer a need.

The situation is not unlike a garden where the divinely wrought potential is great but awaits a gardener's awareness and devotion. There are congregations like untended patches of ground in which some plants never bear fruit. Others flourish luxuriantly but are allowed to "go to seed"—with badly needed products wasted. The same Spirit who plants gifts calls upon God's people to recognize capacities, draw them forth, and use them in mission. Leadership in this enterprise is likely to be most effective if it is vested in a board or committee that uses proven personnel processes to define needs and discover gifts.

A CASE FOR JOB DESCRIPTIONS

The church that is serious about its mission has many personnel needs. One way to determine exactly what they are is to develop plans in the light of the congregation's purpose, then describe each task that must be performed if particular plans are to be carried out. Such descriptions are called "job descriptions" or "responsibility descriptions." Such a description includes statements about (1) the work to be done (job description) or the output to be expected (responsibility description); (2) the time requirements; (3) the relationships involved (responsibility and authority definitions); (4) performance criteria (the position is being well handled when the following conditions exist); (5) incentives; and (6) qualifications.

It is important to recognize that any advance definition of a position will fall short of complete adequacy. For this reason, it should be understood that by mutual agreement every job description will be continually subject to review and revision in the light of the concrete situation and the gifts of the worker.

There are at least five reasons for developing a written job description. (1) It offers ground for a decision about accepting a task. The individual can weigh the commitment involved and come to a rational response. His or her prayer for guidance will not be in a vacuum, and the decision, once made, is likely to be sustained. All too often the church's call is voiced hurriedly in a casual conversation or over a telephone without any clear picture of the involvement expected. Some unfortunates have found themselves before congregations, faced with solemn vows which go far beyond any commitment they were prepared to make. The legitimate resentment engendered by an outrage of this sort or by subsequent heaping up of unexpected responsibilities often results in ineffective leadership or gradual withdrawal which could have been avoided by a clear job description. The instrument also provides (2) a useful guide for functioning; and (3) starting point for changing functions to meet individual or group needs, capacities, or goals not at first recognized. Casual arrangements are much harder to change because the parties frequently have different ideas about the original contract and cannot visualize the position clearly in terms of the group purpose. (4) The job description is also a guard against organizational confusion or fruitless conflict; and (5) it offers a sound basis for evaluation and performance appraisal.

Years ago in a seminar on job descriptions, the pastor of a large inner-city parish indicated that the process would not be of any use among his people. They worked daily at simple operations where such instruments were inappropriate. This approach might be acceptable to middle-class folk, but would be only frustrating to all concerned in his church. The instructor agreed that this could very well be true and the discussion ended at that point. Six months later the pastor reported that he had been wrong. Upon return home, he had decided that he could, at least, draw up a job description for himself. In the process, he decided he ought to invite his church school superintendent, a truck driver, to put together a job description for his church assignment. The man responded enthusiastically after he studied the pastor's effort. The superintendent determined that the department superintendents should be encouraged to prepare similar instruments. They agreed and helped their teachers to join in the same enterprise. At the time of the report, the church school, with hundreds of pupils, was functioning as never before. The absentee rate among teachers had been cut from nearly 20 percent to less than 5 percent! The church was using job descriptions for all its positions and was pleased with the results.

Spontaneity does not have to be eliminated by this rational process. If a member is inspired to start an enterprise consonant with the church's purpose but not covered by a job description, the idea may be set forth in a new description and the effort encouraged.

EFFECTIVE RECRUITING AND TRAINING

We have observed that faith and caring, use of authority and leadership style are all key factors in developing a climate favorable to recruiting. New members should be able to see that Christian faith is finding expression in meaningful activity significantly related to the church's mission and that participants are enthusiastic and fulfilled. They should recognize that persons are called to functions within their capacities and offered means of attaining essential knowledge and skills. They should know that men and women like themselves are performing effectively and will welcome them to a fellowship providing stimulus toward growth and mutual support. They should be encouraged to reflect on the biblical assurance that each member has gifts from the Holy Spirit, who is likely to activate them through a call from the church.

A policy of development will help churches and individuals to avoid frustration and disappointment. Members may be called at first to modest tasks, then advanced to more demanding functions. For example, places on policy-making boards may be reserved for those who have served for several years in tasks that have taken them into many homes of the congregation. Again, a substantial number of new members may be included in projects of limited duration, like evangelistic visitations, every-member canvasses, world mission convocations, religious art festivals, and social action projects—always with careful introductions to the theology and practices involved.

Information may be collected in a personnel file. This will include facts about members who are performing services in the church or community, or have demonstrated gifts in past service, or seem to have dormant talents. The data may come from observations by members of the personnel committee, through their conversations with board and committee members, and with those who visit in homes of the congregation.

Some churches use "time and talent surveys," with cards on which members are asked to record past and present activities and current interests. The survey may be initiated with a thorough training of visitors who will call on every member with a card to be filled out. Thereafter, new members are asked to give answers on a card at the time they are received. Sometimes all the entries are made by interviewers rather than by the members themselves. This may reduce the tendency of individuals to be reticent about their abilities and interests, but it will not eliminate this liability of the survey method, or the risk that a troublesome few may claim nonexistent abilities. A further problem is the adverse reaction which arises when a person indicates interest in an activity but is not invited to participate for a long time because there are no vacancies—or through neglect.

One church arranges for groups of new members to meet, soon after their reception, in the home of an officer. Slides of current activities are shown. Discussion and refreshments follow. After the new members go home, several members of the personnel committee remain and record on cards what they have learned and their plans for cultivating the gifts of the new members. This informal approach has been so successful that they are now inviting groups of inactive members to similar gatherings.

Information handling is not difficult in a congregation of modest size, where it may be largely in the heads of the committee members or in a simple alphabetical file. Larger churches may find it useful to have a key-sort file which allows for quick access to classified capabilities. A few large churches may rent computer time. The time and expense of elaborate information handling should be weighed carefully against the use of the same resources in personal pastoral contacts.

Invitations to serve should be given by two persons, never by telephone. A written job description should be offered together with an explanation of the basis for the call to serve, the reasons for the individual's nomination, and whether the offer is of appointment or to stand for election.

An alternative plan is to offer calls to serve at meetings gathered for the purpose. A group of persons which the committee or organization wishes to call is invited by mail, with a telephone follow-up if necessary. The invitation may be for lunch or dinner or an evening at the church "to deal with a subject of great importance." The host will be the chairperson of the personnel or nominating committee. Officers of the board, committee, or organization, and the pastor will be present. There will be a verbal presentation with a distribution and review of job descriptions, and a few enthusiastic comments from current workers. The chairperson will ask the invited candidates to give an answer privately at the end of the meeting or by telephone within a week. The advantages of this plan include the certainty of a good presentation, group enthusiasm, and demonstration of the quality of persons involved. The major disadvantage is that when there are refusals, a second group must be invited.

General announcements of the need for recruits and especially importunate invitations to volunteer tend to downgrade the tasks and often elicit responses from unqualified persons. It is significant that there is no indication in the New Testament that persons were asked to volunteer.

Refusals to serve should be taken seriously by the personnel committee. About one person in five dislikes group activity but may undertake individual responsibility. Further, active interest in group activity tends to increase with each year of formal education and to decrease after the fiftieth birthday. This may be due, in part, to the kinds of activity offered by the church and community. The committee may discover new opportunities for service attractive to those with limited education and to older persons.

Pleas of community involvement as a reason for refusing tasks in the church may suggest that the church needs a policy which includes community assignments among the concerns of the personnel committee and communicates the conviction that such calls may be from the Holy Spirit. This would mean that members would be encouraged to serve in both the gathered and dispersed activities of the church and to undertake major assignments in either area at different times.

An educational program designed to provide or increase the needed knowledge or skill will encourage people to accept responsibility more readily. It will also increase the likelihood that they will perform effectively.

Newly elected or appointed leaders and workers may be encouraged to read a book or two or some articles provided by the church. Visits may be arranged to observe successful operations, or there may be opportunities to talk with experts or successful practitioners. Each may be given a chance to work for a time with an experienced person. The next step is to visit or teach or lead under "live" or taped observation, and to reflect and discuss performance by way of a verbatim record of what was said. Sessions may be possible with a supervisor who knows how to aid persons in self-appraisal. Or there may be a series of meetings with other learners who gather after functioning to exchange experiences and insights and raise questions.

Other educational opportunities may be offered in special classes or in periods during meetings of boards or committees. A group may agree to read and discuss successive chapters of a book. Courses and continuing education events may be available under denominational, ecumenical, or college or seminary auspices.

IMPROVING PERFORMANCE THROUGH SUPERVISION

One of the most effective processes for improving performance is supervision. Exposure to new responsibilities without help of this sort may lead to growth, but all too often it results in activities that do not serve the church's purposes or fall short of the individual's potential. A good supervisor helps us to understand why we do things and how we can more fully utilize our capacities.

Supervision differs from modeling in which the leader incarnates a vision of a whole system, with its ordering of values, attitudes, and goals. The apostle Paul was very much aware of the impact of his modeling on developing leaders (Phil. 3:17; II Thess. 3:9). In this relationship, communication takes place through a long series of person-to-person contacts, off and on the job, in which the learner becomes aware of qualities and convictions which shape the life and work of the leader. This informal give-and-take may be even more important than supervision in the formation of Christian leaders, since it can provide insight into the nature of Christian service as well as motivation for persistence in the discipline it requires. Under fortunate circumstances, the gifts of the leader, the openness of the learner, and the trust that develops between them may enable the learner to find a role model, useful despite the human imperfections and sinfulness of the exemplar—or perhaps even because of them, since the learner cannot expect to escape these limitations. Supervision does not take the place of modeling, but is a more objective process which involves the learner in reflection upon performance in the interest of improving it.

Supervision differs from counseling, which is a helping process that centers on the problems of living. Supervision concentrates on the task (performance supervision) or on the problems encountered in performance (educational supervision).

A clear contract between supervisor and worker is important. Both should know the purpose of their relationship, its style, and what each is to expect of the other. For example, in a church setting it would be possible for a worker to insist at some point on a counseling relationship addressed to the problems of living, which, however useful, would make it comparatively easy to avoid dealing with shortcomings in performance or problems arising in service activities. The problems of living may bulk so large for an individual that performance becomes next to impossible. In such a situation, the original goals of the relationship may be changed by mutual agreement, but it is usually wiser for the supervisor to refer the barely functional person to a professional counselor.

Kinds of Supervision

Performance supervision is designed to assure that organizational purposes are accomplished through effective action.

The first step is a clarification of purpose. What are we

attempting to accomplish, and why? How is this position related to our mission and what are the goals that make it essential?

The second step is the development of a job description. The third step is goal-setting. The supervisor and the worker discuss the job description and agree on goals for a definite period, possibly modifying the job description to include and correspond to statements about the goals. The fourth step is a process of regular review of the worker's activity and its relation to the established goals, with determination of changes that may enable the worker to move effectively toward the goals. At this point, performance supervision is clearly related to educational supervision.

Educational supervision may be furnished by a performance supervisor, and usually it is. However, there is a distinct difference in focus and goals. While the performance supervisor must give primary attention to accomplishment of the organization's mission, the educational supervisor addresses the problems encountered in performance to show the worker how to appraise his or her own performance in the interest of improving it.

Educational supervision begins at the same point as the fourth step in performance supervision. The educational supervisor encourages us to look at our performance. We may be asked to indicate what we are doing and why, or to review our goals, the steps we have taken to reach them, and the progress that has been made— or the failures that confront us. Or we may begin the conversation by presenting a particular problem or frustration that we encountered as we were at work. The supervisor will help us to clarify our perspective by raising questions about our goals and the appropriateness of our actions, by calling attention to aspects of a situation we may have failed to notice. A good supervisor makes us aware of the competencies we have demonstrated, or of important weaknesses which need to be remedied. He or she presses us to reevaluate the persons around us as they relate to our efforts. Questions help us to see alternate ways of working. Insistence on analysis enables us to see and choose constructive courses of action. Encouragement builds confidence and leads us to take advantage of facilities for growth in knowledge and skill.

Educational supervision will be more effective if the worker often presents concrete material for discussion. Included may be (1) written talks, sermons, prayers, or lesson plans; (2) word-for-word reports (verbatims) or process notes from counseling sessions, visits, or administrative activities; (3) descriptions of programs proposed or in progress; (4) pictorial reports (sociograms—see the next chapter) of group processes; and (5) reflective papers.

Styles of Supervision

The directive supervisor tells the worker what to do. This may be appropriate in an emergency or when a worker is new. An inexperienced church school teacher comes to the pastor on Saturday and says: "Joe Davis, who's been in my class, was killed by a drunken driver last night. I have to face the class and its questions tomorrow. What should I do? Is there something I can read in preparation?" Or a deacon calls up to say: "Tom Brouson has walked out on his wife. I've been trying to get them back to church. Now Joan is desperate and wants me to go over to her house to talk. Should I go? What should I say?" Or Martha Supplee sits down and says: "The League of Women Voters has a tense meeting scheduled for tonight. The president and first vice-president are both ill. I have to conduct the meeting and I've never presided before. How can I get ready?" Under circumstances like these, the supervisor may outline a course of action and furnish materials.

I remember with gratitude how Professor Andrew Blackwood helped me prepare to conduct a funeral at my field-education church on short notice. I had never even attended a funeral! He sent me on my way with some pretty specific instructions and a number of passages marked in a service book. This response to desperation was appropriate. It would not have been had I possessed the background and time to get ready on my own. Thus, the pastor who responds regularly to a request for help in preparing a lesson or establishing a program or meeting a problem by telling someone what to do is probably retarding growth. The directive approach may seem relatively simple and safe, but it tends to reduce motivation and inhibit creativity.

The consultative approach involves a maximum effort by the supervisor to involve the worker in responsibility for goals and actions, and in appraisal of his or her own performance in the interest of improving it. From a consultative supervisory interview, the worker goes forth with a self-imposed task, unlike his neighbor who, subjected to directive supervision, emerges with a supervisor-imposed task. This is not to say that the consultative supervisor has no part in the process. He or she is aware of the expectations and limits imposed by the goals of the system within which supervised and supervisor function, and recognizes the obligation to see that these shape patterns of action. The church school teacher who announces that the Bible is no longer relevant to the needs of young people must be challenged. The leader who supports the young adults in distaste for any form of worship must be encouraged to test this view against the norm of the gospel. The youth adviser who thinks that bowling and ice-skating are the only means of grace has to be asked to think again.

The consultative style is not then distinguished by its relation to the context nor by the subjects to be discussed, but by the supervisor's intention and a procedure consistent with it, designed to involve the worker in critical reflection and responsible action. In a typical situation, a worker may report: "This youth group baffles me. No one wants to take leadership. All the kids just want a good time and they expect me to have a new fun experience for them each week." The supervisor responds, "Have you figured out why they are like this?" He or she then encourages the worker to explore the situation, to clarify his or her own goals in the situation in the light of the church's purposes, to review relationships, and to examine some possible courses of action and choose one. The temptation the supervisor must resist is the impulse to analyze the problem for the worker, to offer solutions, or to dictate programs.

Corporate supervision is most suitable for a group of experienced professionals who wish to help one another appraise performance and increase effectiveness. It may be used to some degree where several workers are functioning together under the guidance of one supervisor. Each may gain much from discussion of performance with peers.

A group of pastors may agree to meet regularly to deal with written cases prepared by members of the group. A board or a commission responsible for calling in the homes of members or new neighbors may gather monthly to look critically at their visits. Teachers or youth leaders may bring problems of performance to their peers in regular sessions, occasionally inviting an expert to join them.

BECOMING AN EFFECTIVE SUPERVISOR

Those who are to exercise supervisory responsibilities need some competence in the kinds of work of the persons they supervise. This concern has led some congregations to assign the supervisory responsibility entirely to the pastor. The superior competence of some members in particular areas is ignored, as is the possibility of special education and training for individuals. Usually, a personnel policy of development opens the way to the choice of supervisory personnel from the ranks, assuring a level of competence in the area at least equal to that of those to be supervised.

Persons with this responsibility very much need practical skill in supervision. One way of obtaining and developing this capacity, once the process is understood, is frequent engagement in supervisory triads. In this exercise, one person presents a problem encountered in performance, a second acts as supervisor, and a third serves as critic. Time periods are established for the supervisory interview and for the criticism. Typical periods may be twenty minutes for the presentation and ten minutes for the critique. After the first round, the roles are changed and the exercise goes on until each participant has tried each role. In seminars we have noted remarkable improvement in supervisory skills as this exercise has been repeated a number of times with different persons in the triads.

Essential in a supervisor of persons engaged in Christian ministry or service is the ability to encourage reflection on tasks in the light of the Bible, the long experience of the church, and the careful thought about God's revelation of himself in Christ which is called "theology." Christians usually recognize the need for this capacity in those who preach and teach, but if the vigorous activities of the church are to be more than a sort of "St. Vitus dance," they must be grounded in the biblical view of life and directed toward the purposes Christ has chosen for his church. The supervisor is in a strategic position to assure this happy state of affairs, and should be encouraged to prepare well. Since the church has sought and developed biblical and theological qualifications in teachers, it should be possible to achieve as much for supervisors.

A congregation that is serious about its mission should be prepared to arrange and, if need be, finance continuing education for supervisors.

LEARNING TO ASSIGN AND DELEGATE

A leader may choose one of three ways of getting something done: do it, assign it, or delegate responsibility for it. If you do it yourself, you have no personnel problems; but you also give up most of the advantages of belonging to an organization, and you severely limit the size of any project in which you can have a part. Individual action may be appropriate in writing an article or a book, preparing and presenting a sermon or a lesson, meeting some decisions or moderating a meeting. It is subversive and frustrating when used in projects involving a number of operations in which others may have equal or superior competencies, especially if you are equipped—as they are not—to perform other needed services.

Assigning tasks widens the leader's scope and clears time for leadership functions. The job description is a satisfactory way of assigning tasks and offers a model for simpler day-to-day assignments which should spell out the work to be done, the time schedule, relationships, and performance criteria. This approach is useful when a worker is new or the operation requires limited creativity.

Delegating is designed to bring into the service of an organization the best a worker can do. By this process, responsibility is shared, authority is given, and accountability is established. A leader or a policy-making group, by delegation, shares responsibility with a chosen person (Ex. 18:13–26; Luke 10:1–3). This in no way diminishes the group's responsibility for the accomplishment of the objective. The failure of the delegated individual is the group's failure—just as his or her success is their success too. What is delegated is the obligation to achieve a result together with license to approach it in the way that seems best. This is quite different from assignment to a task. The responsibility description is a means of delegation and offers a model for less formal or day-to-day delegating. We have noted that this instrument differs from the job description. It replaces the work and time allocations with a statement of responsibility for certain results or the fulfillment of specified goals or objectives. The section on relationships specifies the authority given and the accountability established.

Authority differs from responsibility in that it is not shared in most instances, but transferred. This transfer increases the risk of the leader or group which gives the authority. The temptation is to use assignment instead —or worse, to confer authority and then act as if it had not been given. Thus, a pastor may too easily intervene after a decision is made by a teacher or an officer. A board may reverse a position taken by a musician who acted within delegated authority. A leader may try to change the report of a task force that has worked hard on its assignment. It is important to see that the delegation of responsibility and the accompanying gift of authority, while it does increase risk, also broadens the base of initiative and creative effort.

Discipline which assures that effort will move toward the group's goals is provided by insistence upon *accountability.* This keeps delegating from becoming a laissez-faire approach. It is made clear at the outset that while there is complete freedom in seeking the goal or objective, the process is to be described and justified in some detail to those who did the delegating. In a Christian's activities, this is complicated by a feeling of accountability to God, and when the individual is a professional, by a sense of obligation to peers who alone can judge the level of performance. A sorting out of accountabilities helps. To God, one owes faithful obedience; to peers, professional competence; to an organization of which one is a part, the best possible effort to meet the goals for which responsibility has been assumed. If there is conflict among these accountabilities, it should be examined and resolved before one accepts a particular responsibility, or as soon as it appears.

The process involved in fulfilling a responsibility takes shape or is reformed in one of three ways: other-directed, self-directed, or system-directed.

There is an *other-directed* operation if the person or group that delegated the responsibility tells the worker at the beginning or later just how to reach the goal. Under these circumstances, the delegation is hard to distinguish from assignment. It is, of course, possible that the worker desires this—and even calls upon a performance supervisor to tell just what ought to be done. This request may come either by direct inquiry or by failure to prepare for accountability interviews any clear analysis of the situation with alternate possibilities and preferences. It is also possible that the other—clothed with some authority—may be inclined to tell the worker what to do instead of helping him or her, as a good supervisor should, to see the program critically and develop effective procedures.

The worker is more likely to grow and to be motivated toward maximum effort when involved in *self-directed* activities. Both the delegator and the worker can develop the practice of self-direction by the worker. It is easier when both understand its importance and work toward it, but either can increase the likelihood of its emergence. The delegator, by eliciting information and drawing out ideas and encouraging faltering initiative, may stimulate even the most limited worker toward self-direction. The worker, by preparing analyses and a succession of possibilities with priorities, may persuade even the most authoritarian leader to allow space for self-direction.

System-directed activities are appropriate for routine operations in which the work of several persons overlaps. When a church has several individuals making calls in hospitals or on shut-ins, some arrangement to avoid duplication of effort frees all involved. When different groups are likely to be in a building at the same time, room assignments and rules for behavior benefit all. When materials are to be secured, distributed, shared, stored, or mailed, some generally understood procedures are essential. The time and energy saved by system-directed activities make it worthwhile for all who work in organizations to accept the modest limitations they impose on themselves by adopting them.

PERFORMANCE APPRAISAL ENCOURAGES GROWTH

Performance appraisal at its best makes an individual aware of the quality and quantity of his or her work and provides directions and incentives for improvement. This has obvious advantages for both the worker and the organization.

The evaluation of Christian leadership is as difficult as any performance appraisal, but has the added problem that God is recognized as the final judge. The difficulties introduced by this consideration may be reduced by sorting out accountabilities. Any organization, including the church, would be presumptuous to suppose it could deal with the relation to God's standards of a member's work or as yet unrevealed effects of that activity known only to Deity. Instead, the appraisal is addressed to the Christian's performance in activities designed to accomplish purposes and goals established by the church to which the member has made a commitment in accepting a responsibility.

Under these circumstances, the difficulties connected with performance appraisal in the church are the same as those encountered everywhere. No one wants to appraise another's work. Each dislikes being a critic, remembering all too well Jesus' comic picture of the man with a stick in his eye (Matt. 7:3–4). There is uneasiness, too, about attaining objectivity and making valid judgments. There is discomfort about an assumed superiority which appears on the surface of such an enterprise. The result of all of this is that evaluation of performance occurs to only a limited extent in any organization except when it is forced, as in the military. When it does happen, it is frequently halfhearted. Douglas McGregor reported an industrial study in which 90 percent of the workers said they thought performance appraisal was a good idea but had never experienced it. Yet 40 percent of those in the sample had previously signed an annual statement that their work had been appraised![29]

Further, appraisal that offers an external opinion is of questionable value. Adverse criticism has a largely negative effect on the attainment of goals. Praise seems to have little long-range effect one way or the other.

What does improve performance is goal-setting and review—in consultation. The individual or group is encouraged to establish short-term goals subsidiary to assigned responsibilities. Periodically, the leader prepares for a meeting with a supervisor by reviewing responsibilities and work that has been done, and by comparing results with goals. Then strengths and weaknesses are assessed. The third step is development of specific ways for reaching goals in the next period. This should include plans for remedying deficiencies. At this point, a supervisor can raise questions about objectivity and help the individual see his or her work in the context of a whole enterprise and from a different perspective. In the interest of a wider viewpoint, the supervisor may help in the development of a few questions to be submitted to some of those working with or served by the individual. When the answers are returned, with or without identification of the respondents, they may be discussed in a subsequent interview.

Most people undertaking self-appraisal will welcome guidance in preparing written material. The form made available might include the following instructions:

> Deal with each responsibility in two brief paragraphs. In the first, describe your goals, the activities you have undertaken to reach them, and the results. In the second paragraph, indicate your goals for the period just ahead, your evident strengths, the areas that call for further growth on your part, plans for your development, and why they are appropriate. When this process has been completed for each of your major responsibilities, you may find it useful to examine your use of time by making a diagram of a typical week. Next, you may review your relationships with associates and the persons you serve, and note plans for improving them. Finally, you may examine how you feel about the organization of which

you are a part, and note how you think it could be improved.

The use of self-appraisal—with a modest amount of feedback from others—is superior to other methods. The essential information is available to the individual in a degree not accessible to any supervisor. The focus is on performance rather than on irrelevant personal factors, and it is on the future, about which something can be done, rather than on the unchangeable past. Positive attention is given to strengths and potentials, and there is an attitude which assumes the possibility of greater usefulness, and emphasizes means of growth. The supervisor and the worker are spared some of the resistance to performance appraisal because both recognize that it can help them move toward group goals and individual satisfactions.

THE MULTIPLE STAFF

A congregation's mission frequently requires calling more than one person to give all or a major portion of his or her time to its enterprise. Their relationships will have a great deal to do with their effectiveness and will also, for good or ill, serve as examples for other groups at work in the church. In dealing with this subject, we are indebted to a superb book by Kenneth R. Mitchell, *Psychological and Theological Relationships in the Multiple Staff Ministry.*[30]

The staff may include a minister, a musician, and a sexton—or it may, as size and complexity of mission require, involve a number of professionals and other workers of all sorts.

The shape of their association needs at least four dimensions: a common faith, a covenant, a Christian community, and regular consultation.

A *common faith* does not have to include detailed agreement about all the implications of the gospel, but it does require a united devotion to Jesus Christ as Son of God, Savior, and Lord, and consensus about the nature and purpose of the church and its ministry. When any member of the team regards its primary mission with alien or skeptical eyes, the impact of the whole staff is weakened.

A *covenant* clearly defines goals and procedures for redefining goals. It provides for leadership functions and definitions of responsibility, authority, and accountability. It may take shape in a series of responsibility or job descriptions. Without it, there is the ever-present danger that different members of the group will have unexpressed and contradictory views about what is expected of them—which can repeatedly surface in frustrating conflicts or duplication of effort. Anyone who has engaged in marriage counseling knows how often partners, through inadequate preparation, hold conflicting ideas about the implications of their contract which lead to poisonous resentments. In staff relations, as in marriages, a covenant understood by all parties is essential.

Christian community or *koinonia* will never be perfect on this earth, but there must be conscious effort to establish it among members of a staff. Their fellowship should be actively responding to the divine love by relating in love to God, to one another, and to the world.

The love for God will be expressed in common prayer and praise and service to his children. It may be nurtured by joint study of the experience of the church and the reflection of theologians. The love for one another will be shown in valuing each person for his or her uniqueness, as well as for talents and contributions. It will lead to open communication, unafraid of honesty because of an atmosphere of mutual respect and ready forgiveness. It will be expressed in ever-present support and encouragement in growth. The love for the world will be active in enabling mutual nurture and witness that unites evangelism and efforts for justice and caring relationships among all whom God has made.

Consultation on a regular basis opens the way for effective planning, coordination of effort, management of time sequences, evaluation, and dealing with negative aspects of relationships.

Some pastors try to handle these things as "Lone Rangers," overwhelming themselves with work and frustrating their associates. Others attempt to develop consultative processes but live in constant unexplained tension with fellow workers because they and one or another of the individuals around them are at levels of personal development which are not complementary.

Failures of consultative efforts sometimes arise from aspects of a person's character so far untouched by baptism. Mutual prayer may help, but hardly anything can be more maddening than a person who is conspicuously prayerful and loving but either hides true motivations under unctiousness or—with the best will in the world

—hurts people through ignorance of processes or lack of skill. A leader who becomes aware of turmoil among those around him or her would be well advised to seek out an educational supervisor or a consultant who will spend some time on the scene and have a succession of supervisory interviews with the leader. An alternative is to attend a seminar on leadership where our way of relating will come under scrutiny. An official board faced with a staff problem can tactfully introduce a program of performance appraisal.

However, it is well to remember that our examination of decision-making suggested that the consultative approach need not always imply a contract to follow a consensus or a majority vote. There may be areas in which a staff covenant should allocate decisions to an individual, following advice from the group.

THE OFFICIAL BOARD

Most of this chapter has been devoted to processes that may be used by all members as they seek to work together. There should be insights of particular value to those with leadership responsibilities. The corporate life of the church staff may have a shaping impact on all the groups in the congregation. Since this may be true in a unique degree of the life and service of the official board members, it is suggested that the reader review the four dimensions discussed under "The Multiple Staff" and think of them as referring to the official board. Suggestions about the operation of board meetings appear in the next chapter, but this material is basic.

The most important event in the life of our congregation this year may well be a weekend retreat for the official board. There we can explore together our common faith, renew our working covenant, deepen our sense of community, and develop better ways of consulting with one another.

9

Meetings and Church Groups

Meetings have held an important place in the life of the church from the beginning. Our Lord gathered people into groups wherever he went and regularly presided over meetings of the Twelve. He brought them together to discuss things he had said and done, to receive instructions for projects, to hear of his plans and learn to appreciate and forgive each other. On the night he was betrayed, he sat with the Twelve around a table and he kept them around him as he prayed in the Garden of Gethsemane. He urged the disciples to meet together regularly after the resurrection and promised he would be spiritually present in their midst. It was when they were meeting together that the Holy Spirit gave them power and direction. Thereafter, they gathered with the assurance that the place to expect the guidance of the Spirit was the meeting. (Matt. 18:20; cf. Matt. 5:1ff.; 13:10, 36; 16:6–20; 17:19–21; 18:1–20; 26:20–46; Acts 1:1–8; 2:1ff.; 13:1–3; 15:1ff.)

In all of this, our Lord stood squarely in the mainstream of Judaism, which had discovered in a hostile environment the value of the small believing group. During the Babylonian exile and under Roman oppression these units proved effective in establishing community of faith, eliciting commitment, sharing knowledge and understanding, and developing creativity. They accomplished what no individual could do alone, fostering religious identity and development.

WE CANNOT DO WITHOUT MEETINGS

Meetings can waste time, sometimes on a grand scale. Most of us have been caught in well-meaning but fruitless gatherings. We appreciate the jokes that express impatience at the wordy pretensions and small productivity of committees, boards, and task forces. We are tempted to despise meetings and declare our independence—but we cannot do alone what may be accomplished by a team. Meetings are essential.

A community of faith can only come into being in a meeting, and it can only maintain itself in a succession of meetings. Those present belong. They share convictions and in a subtle way their lives intertwine. Part of the meaning of each one's activity is found in the activity of the others. Different members satisfy their own needs in the interaction in a variety of ways, but all find some of their meaning in the group goal. If the mutual convictions and the group goal are petty, the meeting will not amount to much; but if convictions and goal are worthy, the meeting can be the beginning or the continuation of a real community.

A meeting may also elicit *a level of commitment* rarely developed in any other environment. We have seen the central importance of participation to motivation. When a person spends an evening with others in planning an evangelistic effort or a stewardship campaign or a social action project, that person is more likely to put his or her person or money or vote on the line when the action begins. Most pastors and officers have also experienced the kind of loyalty that springs up among those who meet regularly. It is notable that Judas left the upper room early. Jesus gave him an easy "out" which was also a last appeal, but it is probable that he could not have gone through with his betrayal had he stayed to the end (John 13:21–30).

Knowledge and understanding exchanged in meetings are indispensable for most complex enterprises. Some of the essential exchange may occur in letters, memos, and conversations, but where teamwork is important there is no adequate substitute for the communication that occurs in a meeting. Members carry about information that others need to do their part well. It is only in the give-and-take about what they are doing or want to do that participants draw out what others know. Often, the information is already at hand but the perspectives of others set it in a new light.

Meetings lead to *corporate accomplishment.* They bring together individuals endowed with a variety of the gifts of the Spirit. However richly endowed each person may be, it is usually possible for them to achieve things, by teamwork, that would be beyond the capacity of any one person. Nor is this merely the result of adding what each has done and ascribing the total to the group. From meetings emerge accomplishments that would never have seen the light of day without the multiplying effect of the group experience.

Meetings also play a crucial part in *developing creativity.* Members are stimulated to fresh thinking when immediate feedback indicates that a cherished idea is unattractive or unintelligible to others. Minds begin to race when an urgently needed solution eludes the whole group. The emergence of an original idea challenges members to weigh it against other possibilities, spot its strengths and weaknesses, and, if necessary, improve it. Evidence from areas as different as medical research and artists' colonies suggests that even genius is more likely to be creative under group stimulation, and pedestrian individuals together may be capable of unusual creativity.

Meetings have extraordinary *power to change persons.* Experiments during World War II indicated conclusively that a succession of three or four meetings with free interaction were far more effective than an equal number of lectures or personal interviews in developing new patterns of behavior. The result in this experiment was not due to manipulative actions by which one reaches over the mind of the individual to touch the springs of behavior. It was due, first, to the better communication possible in a group in which feedback of misunderstandings opens the way to immediate corrections. The changed behavior was rational once the situation was fully understood. Second, the group supported its members in the difficult effort to maintain the new and more rational behavior. The implication is clear that when the church has a sound pattern based on a gospel imperative, there is no stronger ally in establishing it in the lives of the people than the regular meeting. That this is not a new insight is borne out by the practice of Jesus, as of the prophets before him with their "schools." The saints have honored him ever since with their circles of disciples, monastic communities, prayer meetings, retreats, and personal groups of all sorts.

FACTORS THAT AFFECT GROUP RELATIONS

The ideal *size* for the functions we have been discussing is a group of twelve or fewer. As a group increases in number beyond twelve, the essential communication becomes more and more difficult and much of the business appropriate to small-group process is best delegated to committees or task forces. Boards of up to thirty-five or forty members may effectively pool knowledge, make decisions, and develop commitment. To do this they must depend on smaller subgroups for preparing materials, sharpening issues, community building, creativity, and stimulation of personal growth. Assemblies of much larger size may still be centers of communication and perform essential decision-making functions. They may even foster commitment to the extent to which they are able to provide for real participation of members. Very large meetings can do some things that small groups cannot accomplish. They can produce a magnificent service of divine worship through which members can help one another express their love and praise, or establish a project of wide scope which requires energy from many dedicated lives.

Most of the processes examined in this chapter have their primary location in small groups, though, as we have seen, they may have important effects upon large assemblies as subgroups deal with much of their business.

A group meets for some purpose and it is useful to clarify the purpose at the outset. The intention may be primarily communicative and informative: the sharing or discovery of knowledge. While it takes longer, a meeting assures a kind of personal interchange which cannot be effected by any other form of communication. More often, a meeting is called to make decisions about policy or about implementation of policy.

Those who have studied what goes on in meetings refer to the stated intention of a meeting as *the public agenda.* It is usually not hard to clarify the group purpose. An official board meets to decide about admissions to membership or program development. A committee meets to plan or carry out a program.

Observers have noticed that alongside the public agenda in any group there will be what they call *the hidden agenda.* This is not a secret scheme to exploit or manipulate the company. It is, rather, a way of talking about the individual needs and desires of the members which inevitably affect the way they deal with everything that comes up in a meeting. We have seen that organizations simultaneously meet group goals and individual needs and desires, and this is clearly a feature of meetings.

Years ago I saw a film in which a dozen persons sat around a table discussing juvenile delinquency in their small town. Severe vandalism concerned every one of them: the police chief, the school principal, several storekeepers, the mayor, and a number of parents. After about fifteen minutes of spirited discussion, the picture began to repeat itself. This time, however, as the same dialogue was given again, it was interrupted as cones of light disclosed other persons behind each of the participants. We could hear what those ghosts whispered among themselves and to the public participants. A storekeeper's wife wrung her hands as she spoke to him and their son of their resources depleted by theft and broken plate glass just when the youth was ready for college. The police chief's wife urged moderation since their son was secretly one of the culprits. All around the table were human explanations of the dialogue that had not been obvious when one concentrated only on the group purpose. The hidden agenda was having a potent effect on the public agenda.

Group functioning is also affected by *physical conditions.* Every experienced leader is aware of the importance of physical details such as ventilation, temperature, and light. Room size can be important. A small company meeting in a great cavernous room, or seated in a corner of a vast space, will usually deal with its task more effectively if relocated within dimensions related to its size. One youth group that had tried to conduct its business in a large, bare hall became a different fellowship when permitted to use the well-furnished church parlor. An official board, accustomed to cramped, ill-ventilated quarters, seemed to change character when it began to meet in an airy space where there was room for everyone to be seated around a square table.

There will be more participation in a meeting when those present face one another around a table or in an informal circle. Seating people in rows so that they are unable to see faces impedes communication. Since increased distance also tends to impair communication, there is an obvious difficulty when a group is large. One solution is to place seats in concentric circles, but this should be necessary only when the membership exceeds thirty-five or forty. A satisfactory gathering place for up to forty board members can be arranged by placing chairs around the outside of a square of eight of the ten-foot oblong tables used for dining in most churches.

People approach a group task with less distraction from the public agenda when seated at a table where papers and note pads may be conveniently located, and body language (which may be embarrassingly revealing of personal feelings) is not so completely exposed as it is in a lounge chair circle. The shape of the seating arrangement also affects the social relationships. A long narrow table prevents some of the members from seeing or hearing others, and if the leader sits at one end, relegates some to second-class positions. Furthermore, it is worth a good deal of effort to arrange that everyone present be seated in the circle and not outside it or behind the others. A person left out by inadequate arrangements or individual preference may feel disengaged and may resort to obstructive behavior.

The social atmosphere of a meeting may contribute substantially to its success. Name tags increase the possibility of direct personal address in dialogue. They should include both first and last names in letters at least one inch high and of the solid substance made possible by the heavy markers now available. The best base is the 5″ × 8″ card, folded lengthwise in half. It may be lettered on both sides and placed on the table in front of the individual, or on the floor if the circle is without tables. The gummed or pinned labels in frequent use are less satisfactory but may be useful if the lettering is bold and the group is small.

CREATING A WORKING GROUP

Team-building exercises are worthwhile if the group is to work together for some time. One approach has proved invaluable in opening a new level of relationship among church board members. Each is asked to write down on an 8½″ × 11″ sheet of paper brief descriptions of three deeply satisfying experiences, one from childhood, one from youth, and one from adulthood—with the understanding that these will be discussed with others. If the group is small, the next hour is devoted to a report on the three items from each member who responds to questions and joins in discussion. If the group is large, the members spend fifteen minutes briefly examining each other's sheets, then each chooses one other member with whom he or she would enjoy further exchange. These two choose two others until subgroups of six are formed. The subgroups spend the next hour exchanging experiences. After this exercise, the people around the table look at one another in a new way. Their relationship is no longer that of a collection of unknown quantities who happen to be interacting in pursuit of goals. It is much more likely that mutual understanding and trust will develop—setting the stage for simultaneous task accomplishment and personal growth.

The church, like most other human institutions, has long been aware of the team-building values of meals together and the enhancement of relationships that occurs when a group participates in an overnight retreat or conference. The extended time allows people opportunity to play together and talk of experiences and in-

terests and convictions, and to become real to each
other. The leader who does not encourage church
groups to develop these possibilities is throwing away
valuable resources.

The leader also has responsibility for *modeling trust,*
which is the essential atmosphere for a group working
together. When an ordered body such as a church board
or committee is trying to supply corporate leadership,
every member has an obligation to increase the level of
trust. This means seeing in each of the others the full
potential of a creative child of God, and expecting respect for confidentiality. It also involves giving others
the same credit for good intentions assumed of one's
self. Further, it includes taking seriously the hard work
of task forces and not demanding that committee work
be redone by the larger body.

Relative positions developed in the course of group
process affect everything that goes on, and it is worthwhile for the group to know what to expect. After people have worked together for a time, they tend to
evolve status patterns. Certain individuals are expected
to behave in fairly predictable ways and others to respond to them along familiar lines. Some engage in
"pairing," with an inclination to back each other on any
issue, while some "square off," always contesting each
other's positions. One here and another there regularly
depend upon a particular member and will support him
or her. Some members deal with proposals they find
objectionable by fighting them every step of the way;
others retreat into silence, only expressing opposition
by a vote—or later, through informal means.

Securing acceptance in a group may be more difficult
than it looks. A newcomer disturbs well-established re-

lationships. Since belonging is of prime importance to all human beings, the introduction of a stranger can be threatening. A leadership role that involves risks but should be undertaken by every member is that aimed at drawing in new members.

Years ago, a youth group on retreat had in its midst an obese young woman who had never participated before. Throughout the first day she was left out of everything that happened. The adult advisers called this to the attention of the fellowship executive committee. The young leaders expressed concern and three of the girls agreed to work for her inclusion. In the early afternoon, everyone emerged from cabins and started for the beach about a thousand feet away. The stout girl was in the center but she moved at a slow pace which gradually allowed a gap to develop between her (and the three girls who resolutely walked beside her) and the large group. As we watched from the porch of the main lounge, the gap widened and the three good Samaritans grew more and more tense, until one could stand it no longer. She broke and ran to catch up with her comrades. A few minutes later, the second girl said something and dashed off. The third held on for a little longer, then gave up and ran to close ranks with her friends. I think of this scene often as I watch the strain that develops when church members attempt to make newcomers welcome—with one eye on established friends they do not wish to miss. A more subtle drama occurs in church boards when newly elected members attend for the first time. Some team-building effort should be used on such occasions.

The pressures to conform in any group are strong because of the human need for belonging. As we have seen, these pressures may be allies of learning and growth and accomplishment. They may also be used to manipulate persons into taking positions or doing things abhorrent to their reason or convictions. In an extreme case, a graduate student who was absent one week from class was the following week made to believe that he had seen things in a motion picture that were not in the film and that things he had seen were not in the picture. The conspiracy was maintained for so long that when they informed him what had been done, he could not accept their statements until he was shown the film again. Such possibilities place a great responsibility for integrity on all participants in group process. They suggest that groups, like official boards, should find time to explore together what is known about group dynamics.

IMPROVING GROUP PERFORMANCE

It should be particularly useful to be aware of the leadership roles that must be exercised if a group is to accomplish its purposes.

Achieving the group task depends on the assumption by some person or persons of certain responsibilities. Initiating is one. Goals or next steps must be proposed; problems defined; procedures suggested. Seeking and giving information is essential; so is offering feedback. Clarifying may be done by asking questions; restating, dividing, or uniting a proposal; summarizing the position as it emerges from debate; or proposing consensus testing.

Maintenance-oriented roles keep the group at its task, and deal with hidden agendas representing personal needs and desires. Listening opens the way to awareness of various agendas, and interpreting them in relation to the group goals. Encouraging mutual trust may come about through expressions of acceptance of persons. Careful questions may offer opportunity for expressions of feeling which must be heard before individuals can give attention to the group agenda. Harmonizing may involve asking those who reject a view to state it, to the satisfaction of an opponent, before attacking. Sometimes it is useful to suggest compromises. "Gatekeeping" requires efforts to see that every member has a part in the discussion, often by asking questions of quiet members, calling attention to someone who has tried in vain to get the floor, or saying to a talkative member in a pause: "John, I think we see what you are driving at. Could we find out what Lois is thinking about this?"

The board or committee may be interested in a picture of its deliberations which emerges when one member is asked to make a sociogram. This shows the position of each participant, with an arrow drawn each time a person speaks, pointing to the person addressed or to the center when the whole group is addressed. Such a diagram shows plainly just what is happening and is one of the best ways of reminding some members that they have an obligation to draw out others and develop a more participative group.

An observer may also be asked to record who makes what kinds of contributions in terms of such task and maintenance responsibilities as we have mentioned. Another interesting observer's report may deal with the general atmosphere (formal or informal, cooperative or competitive, supportive or hostile, interested or apathetic), goals (clear or vague, based on solid theological norms?), or accomplishments. It may also be illuminating to list the important functions of church meetings explored in the beginning of this chapter and have the entire group discuss which of them should have been fulfilled and what actually happened.

Group facilitation should never be allowed to become a major preoccupation, much less an end in itself. But early attention to the processes involved may greatly increase the yield of the time spent in meetings.[31]

LEADING A BUSINESS MEETING

In preparing for a business meeting, the leader should clarify its purpose, assure the development of a proposed agenda and, if possible, circulate it in advance. In setting the order of presentations, the leader should remember that the early part of the time tends to be more lively and creative—or, possibly, more contentious. Most meetings drag after two hours. Church boards and committees can, and should, learn to complete their business within that span of time. This involves discipline. Those who have items for consideration should submit brief background papers to be distributed in advance with the agenda. They should also agree to a time allotment. In most churches, this is best worked out by an agenda committee or an executive committee which meets with the pastor and the secretary of the board. When it is obvious that there will not be time for all the business, low-priority items may be docketed for the following month—or, very occasionally, a major issue may call for a special meeting. The closing time should be stated on the proposed agenda, with time allotments suggested for each item.

Time should be allocated at the beginning for adjustments or changes so that everyone has some ownership of the schedule. Care should be taken to assure that the agenda or executive committee and the other committees prepare issues for decision, but do not attempt to preempt the decision-making power of a board.

The minutes of a meeting should indicate its date, time, and place. The names of all present should be listed, and the excuses of absentees. (This encourages attendance.) Agenda items and their disposition should be recorded, together with an indication of the person or group responsible for implementation. The date, time, and place of the next meeting should be included, with a final note giving the adjournment time.

The chairperson ought to see that individuals and groups carry out their responsibilities, developing patterns of action if these were not established in the meeting, and following a workable time frame. He or she will want, as soon as possible, to go over with particular members their plans for presentation at the next meeting.

Where a pastor is included in a meeting, he or she should explore the extent to which the group meets purposes suggested by the New Testament for the church, and individual needs legitimated by biblical views. It may also be essential to ask what personal or family needs emerged that should be approached in terms of pastoral care. Other members of the group may soundly conclude that they share the pastor's obligations in these areas, and in consultation with him or her, may undertake some of the efforts implied.

MEETINGS SMALL AND LARGE

Each member of a church should have access to membership in a small group in order to develop a close relationship with some other Christians. These groups may be designed for Bible study, prayer, and exchange of personal experience, with some provision for community action that will keep the fellowship from becoming self-centered. They may be primarily study groups or work groups or recreation groups. They may be inclusive of both sexes and all ages, or appeal to persons of a particular status or need. They may be for youth, or young adults, or older people, or alcoholics, or single parents, or couples. It is important that they be kept small so that the members come to know one another well, to support one another in growth and in crises, and may—if they wish—meet in one another's homes. For persons in most of the categories suggested, groups of more than twenty-five are a waste of time; and a better size is usually a dozen persons or couples.

In organizing small groups, one must remember that at least twenty percent of the population prefer not to hold membership in small groups. Pressure to join will only alienate them. For the rest, the experience can be fruitful. Leaders can be helpful in responding to requests for establishing new categories of groups, or launching work projects, and in making persons aware of options.

Large meetings have their uses in bringing together rich resources for worship. They also provide arrangements for decisions that affect a large number of persons or shape structures and programs for extensive geographical areas. They serve the church well. But the church is not a meeting; it is a fellowship of persons, the family of God. The church is every bit itself in dispersion, with members at work throughout society, as in a small group gathered in worship or mutual nurture or reconciling mission. However, the large gathering may inspire and encourage the faithful on occasion. It may even provide a foretaste of that family reunion when a great multitude of all nations and people and kindred and tongues gathers in final triumph before the throne of God and the Lamb (Rev. 7:9).

Notes

1. J. Douglas Brown, *The Human Nature of Organizations* (American Management Association, 1973), pp. 22–26.

2. Bob Woodward and Carl Bernstein, *All the President's Men* (Simon & Schuster, 1974).

3. Most centers of continuing education offer these experiences. The National Training Laboratories, connected with the National Education Association, Washington, D.C., offer a wide variety of groups and have a program for certifying leaders.

4. Kenneth Mitchell, *Psychological and Theological Relationships in the Multiple Staff Ministry* (The Westminster Press, 1966), pp. 59–67.

5. Abraham Maslow, *Motivation and Personality* (Harper & Brothers, 1954).

6. M. Scott Myers, "Who Are Your Motivated Workers?" *Harvard Business Review,* January 1964, pp. 73–88.

7. Douglas McGregor, *The Human Side of Enterprise* (McGraw-Hill Book Co., 1960), pp. 15–57.

8. Amitai Etzione, *Modern Organizations* (Prentice-Hall, 1964), pp. 50–53.

9. Robert R. Blake and Jane S. Mouton, *The Managerial Grid* (Houston: Gulf Publishing Co., 1964), presents a widely used instrument for testing one's orientation. It may be self-administered by a pastor or a board. A copy of the grid with

a set of eighteen questions and full instructions is available for duplication in J. William Pfeiffer and John E. Jones, *A Handbook of Structured Experiences for Human Relations Training*, rev. ed., Vol. I (Universities Associates Press, 1970), pp. 7–11; this handbook is available from Universities Associates Press, P.O. Box 615, Iowa City, IA 52250. Lyle Schaller discusses the possibility of balancing orientations of persons working together in *Survival Tactics in the Parish* (Abingdon Press, 1977), pp. 42–48.

10. See Victor Vroom, "A New Look at Managerial Decision-Making," *Organizational Dynamics*, n.d., pp. 1–15. See also Vroom, "Can Leaders Learn to Read?" *Organizational Dynamics*, Winter 1976, pp. 17–28. The decision-making strategies proposed in outline are related to Vroom's categories.

11. This is a simplification of the statement on p. 13 of the first Vroom article cited above.

12. The Confession of 1967, in *The Book of Confessions*, Part I of *The Constitution of The United Presbyterian Church in the United States of America* (Office of the General Assembly of The United Presbyterian Church U.S.A., 1970), Section 9.31.

13. *Ibid.*

14. Etzione, *op. cit.*, is an excellent resource for those who wish to explore this story in more detail.

15. For more information, see Warren G. Bennis, *Organization Development: Its Nature, Origins, and Prospects* (Addison-Wesley Publishing Co., 1969), and other paperback titles available from Addison-Wesley Publishing Co., Reading, MA 01867.

16. Sometimes the names of very disparate categories are presented as designating competing theories of organization. Included frequently are the names of two of the schools (Classical and Human Relations), along with ways authority is legitimated (Traditional, Charismatic, and Bureaucratic), and a useful model (Systemic). Each is related to a sequence of

behaviors, and these are then evaluated theologically. I am proceeding on the assumption that given the present state of our knowledge it is more realistic and valuable to examine particular organizational activities and processes and test them in the light of our Christian convictions and theological reflection about them.

17. Brown, *op. cit.,* pp. 1, 3, 11.

18. See F. E. Emery (ed.), *Systems Thinking* (Penguin Books, 1969). For an ecclesiastical development of this model, see Alvin J. Lindgren and Norman Shawchuck, *Management for Your Church* (Abingdon Press, 1977).

19. Brown, *op. cit.,* p. 68.

20. Marshall McLuhan, *Understanding Media: The Extensions of Man* (McGraw-Hill Book Co., 1964); see especially pp. 22–32.

21. For an amusing and informative discussion of game theory, see John MacDonald, *Strategy in Poker, Business, and War* (W. W. Norton, 1950).

22. Heraclitus, *The Cosmic Fragments,* ed. by G. S. Kirk (Cambridge University Press, 1954), pp. 17, 106–107.

23. Alvin Toffler, *Future Shock* (Random House, 1970); see especially pp. 289–326. See also, for statistics, the report of Thomas Holmes, professor of psychiatry at the University of Washington, to the American Association for the Advancement of Science; reported in *Time,* March 1, 1971, p. 54.

24. Jürgen Moltmann, *Hope and Planning* (Harper & Row, 1971), p. 183.

25. John Dewey, *How We Think* (D. C. Heath and Co., 1910), pp. 68–78.

26. For more information about this process, see Roderick K. Macleod, "Program Budgeting Works in Nonprofit Institutions," *Harvard Business Review,* September-October 1971, pp. 46–56.

27. The chart may take grid form with steps listed down the left side in vertical sequence, and the dates across the top of the page heading vertical columns. Check marks will show

when each step should be completed; double checks when it is. Sometimes the sequence of steps is simply listed with dates and is referred to as a "flow chart." Occasionally, when there are complex relationships between a number of operations, we use a graph form called a "critical path network." Each task is depicted by a line with dated segments, which intersects with other lines, or branches off on given dates. The network picture encourages us to be realistic about our timing. See R. L. Martino, *Critical Path Networks* (Management Development Institute, 1967).

28. A useful instrument for those working their way through the steps of the planning process is Richard E. Rusboldt, Robert K. Gladden, and Norman M. Green, Jr., *Local Church Planning Manual* (Valley Forge: Judson Press, 1977). The authors are executives of the American Baptist Churches, specializing in leadership development, research, and planning. They approach the subject theologically and practically. There is a wealth of background material and many useful worksheets.

29. Douglas McGregor, "An Uneasy Look at Performance Appraisal," *Harvard Business Review,* September-October 1972, pp. 133–138.

30. Mitchell, *op. cit.*

31. Further reading about group processes may include with profit: Philip A. Anderson, *Church Meetings That Matter* (United Church Press, 1965); and Joseph Luft, *Group Processes,* 2d ed. (National Press Books, 1970). Suggestions about starting and developing groups will be found in John L. Casteel, *The Creative Role of Interpersonal Groups in the Church Today* (Association Press, 1968).

Index

187